CLIMATICA
Forma urbis

n°2

Giovanni Marco Chiri
with texts and images of Ilaria Giovagnorio
Foreword by Mosé Ricci

My initial idea was for this book series to be in one way or another "essential". My opinion was that I could have guided it and developed at least a few of the topics covered in it, only on the condition that it would be truly useful. But useful to whom? Who would really feel the urge to read these short, printed texts? Certainly I didn't, and still don't, have the ambition to contribute substantially to the theory of the project nor to elaborate on themes that are so eccentric that they raise the interest and curiosity of only a few academics in the field. On the other hand, I admit that the mere idea of writing one – or more – strictly educational texts bored me.

Returning to the basis of the discipline and using them to rebuild a way of working has, in a way, a fundamental value and – though this may seem audacious – is highly exciting.

GmC

CLIMATICA. City form
by Giovanni Marco Chiri

With texts and images of Ilaria Giovagnorio

Foreword by Mosé Ricci

foreword
by Mosè Ricci

The simultaneous effects of three key factors – the economic crisis, the environmental emergency and the IT revolution - are rapidly changing our lifestyles and the way we imagine the solid physical form of our future. This is all coming about at time when design knowledge suddenly appears inadequate both as an instrument to interpret the contemporary world and as a device for generating new environmental conditions. Looking to the future, perhaps what is happening to the most advanced societies because of diffuse and shared information is the creation of a chance to live more physical space than ever without having to conform it to specific pre-determined uses. An enormous amount of built volume is available in our cities; much is not used or no uses have yet been defined for it. The same is true of infrastructure and public space.
Therefore for the western world the theme is now to work on the existing built legacies, to regenerate cities giving new life cycles to the built patrimony that already exists. In this sense is the future annulled for architecture and the city? Is the existing city -the present time- our only possible context? The apparent fixity of physical spaces upsets the modernist idea of time? *Modernity is the time in the era in which time has a history* wrote Bauman in 2006 . In the modernity *genius loci* and *genius saeculi* coincide. The society projected its idea of future in the forms of the city, architecture, art and fashion that realized the era.

What is the destiny of architecture (intended as the discipline of design) today in the age that apparently only considers - or at least gives absolute priority to - the evolution of immaterial space and its related mechanisms? When will the increased efficiency and re-signification of existing buildings, as opposed to new construction, become the core issues? Returning to the initial questions, while everything is rapidly changing, buildings and cities apparently remain the same. Is it possible to think about a new statute for the architecture of the eternal present?

Great technological advances have always produced great transformations in styles and forms of living, and as a consequence, in styles and forms of design. One of the main theoretical questions of modernity concerned the best possible synthesis of form and function. With the information technology revolution, today the problem is the opposite: namely to confer meaning, narrative and use - even *pro-tempore*- to spaces that already have form and to transform them into attractive, habitable, and ecologically viable places.

Our era requires new paradigms (as new points of view looking to the future) and a new idea of the design of physical space. Such a challenge could give value to the existing built context deploying conceptual strategies that leverage a shift in meaning and a new lifecycle for habitable space. This challenge considers context as a project and the landscape as infrastructure that produces ecological value; and the future of the city then becomes a collective project rather than an authorial one.

For obvious reasons, society has always been interested in the quality of urban form, and more than ever this has been identified with the environmental, economic and social sustainability of design actions. Aesthetic values remain fundamental but are rapidly changing. Today, innovation in architecture seems to be moving toward the definition of a new theoretical/practical framework based on three main and non-oppositional goals that almost always complement one another: *the project as a narrative, the project as a social action, the project as performance rather than sign*. These three points of view on architecture are expressions of beauty in the city of the eternal present: narration, social action and performance. All of them consider the landscape as new context for action.

The paradigm of the *project as narrative* expresses the need to confer meaning upon the project for the existing context, to reveal what is already there through fresh eyes. Rem Koolhaas expressed this paradigm superbly in his project for the Prada Foundation in Milan by encasing the former industrial warehouse in gold foil. N*arrative architecture*, as Giancarlo De Carlo wrote, *è capace di ascoltare, accogliere, annettere quelle che sono le tensioni della città e dei suoi abitanti. Un'architettura che deve farsi "processo", scardinando la visione consolidata dell'edificio come un unicum perfetto e concluso*[1](Marini, 2013). In the strict etymological sense, the narrative unveils different meanings, tells the story of a building and those who inhabit it through signs of its re-signification. Sometimes citizens themselves or artists are the ones who *write* the stories of the buildings like Dan Pitrera at the Detroit Collaborative Design Center, or Francesco Giorgino, known as Millo, in Turin's mural paintings. More often, the architectural motivation underlying a project can explain the sense of the narrative tension: evocative as in Claudio Lucchini's Hannah Arendt school in Bolzano or anti-rhetorical and pop as in the ski slope for BIG's power plant in Copenhagen.

Design as social action lies at the core of a variety of contemporary works on spaces (even temporary ones) for dwelling and collective transport systems. As mentioned, this is one of the central points of the 2016 Venice Biennale. As Aravena wrote: *"We would like to learn from architectures that despite the scarcity of means intensify what is available instead of complaining about what is missing. We would like to understand what design tools are needed to subvert the forces that privilege the individual gain over the collective benefit, reducing We to just Me. We would like to know about cases that resist reductionism and oversimplification and do not give up architecture's mission to penetrate the mystery of the human condition. We are interested in how architecture can introduce a broader notion of gain: design as added value instead of an extra cost or architecture as a shortcut towards equality"*. Design as social action pertains of course not only to buildings but also to

---

[1]. *"can listen, embrace, annex the tensions of the city and its inhabitants. An architecture has to become "process", undermining the established vision of the building as a perfect and finished whole"*

neighbourhoods, public space and infrastructure. It is achieved as a goal of emancipation, most often through processes of a shared design process rather than participation. Often, in this kind of project, the traditional concept of the "author" is questioned by sharing the creative process while the implementation process is self-managed *hic et nunc*. It overcomes long-winded bureaucratic authorization processes and public licensing. As paradigms of this approach, among others, the works of Alfredo Brillembourg, *Urban Think Tank*, Gravalos' and Di Monte's "Esto non es un Solar" and Boamistura in Brazilian favelas, as well as Italian *guerrilla gardens* can be mentioned.

The *project as performance rather than sign* is the technological paradigm modulated as an operative aesthetic and conceptual principle. Architecture of *performance* versus architecture of *sign* means focusing transformation not on use but on an innovative result, measurable prevalently, but not only, in ecological terms. It is the contemporary evolution of Manuel Gausa's *Advanced Architecture* (2001). This theme can be developed both on the urban level - from the policies for Barcelona's smart city to Copenhagen's bio-city-, and on the architectural and design scale; it can even pertain to process design, as in Carlo Ratti's senseable design lab at the MIT. *"We are facing a change in the field of Architecture, a move towards a different form of "habitats", where architecture is not merely inhabited, but becomes interactive and evolutional; a technologically integrated interface"* remarks Areti Markopoulou, academic director of IaaC (institute for advanced architecture of Catalunya), one of the foremost international schools of architecture, a laboratory for the continuous experimentation of technological innovation. The performative principle brings architecture into a contemporary dimension, transforming it into a terminal (or interface) within a system of physical or immaterial relationships that constitute its essence. It is the re-contextualisation of an idea of design within a space for new, and not necessarily material, actions.

The result of the shift from the aesthetic of the *sign* to that of *meaning* confer beauty to a new form of the city-landscape in which buildings and cities are in harmony with the environment and describe a new landscape. Nature becomes the main infrastructure between linking humans and quality of life; the city is the sensory form of dwelling in a gradually expanding present, growing in size and pace.

Gianmarco Chiri faces these themes in Climatica. To explore the opportunities of design within a framework of the immense environmental challenges facing our generation is the only choice, but it is also innovative. This research needs to be carried out because either architecture will prove to be a resilient discipline – even when enrolment in architecture schools decrease in most western countries, especially in Italy - and find a decisive, sustainable and appropriate role in contemporary life, or it may never be able to halt its decline with the presumption of the unnecessary. It is an innovative choice because the issues driven by the environmental challenge have thus far appeared irrelevant or supplementary, but never paradigmatic - until now.
There was a time in which this was not so, as Gianmarco Chiri points out with extreme clarity. Let us hope that everyone will read this volume and soon follow the lines of research that the author so resolutely delineates and a new *architectural climate*.

index

4
Foreword

12
Sustainability

24
Key concepts

34
Genealogy

50
Pioneers

78
Practices

86
Bibliography

90
Credits

92
Carnet

"Why should I care about future generations? What have they have ever done for me?"

Groucho Marx

CHAPTER ONE

Chapter ONE

Sustainability

The year is 2035.

"In New York, palm trees line the Hudson River from 125th Street to the Midtown exit. Phoenix is in its third week of temperatures over 130 degrees C and the project to cover the city with air-conditioned domes is still unfinished. Holland is under water. Bangladesh has ceased to exist. Torrential rains and rising seas there have killed several million people and forced the remaining population into makeshift refugee camps on higher ground in Pakistan and India. In central Europe and the America Midwest, decades of drought have turned once fertile agricultural lands into parched deserts. Tens of millions of people continue to trek northward the greatest mass migration in recorded history. Canada's population swells from 20 million to 200 million in less than 4 decades. Forest fires rage out of control over millions of acres in the Pacific Northwest, while the Mississippi River, closed to commercial traffic earlier in the century, becomes a vast earthen plain, allowing people to cross over by foot for the first time in human memory. The ozone layer continues to shrink causing a pandemic of cancer deaths. Hundreds of millions of people are exposed to dangerous levels of ultraviolet radiation that compromise their immune system and millions more become vulnerable to a series of new and strange diseases sprouted on irreparable failures and the eradication of the entire ecosystem all over the planet. Welcome to the world of the twenty-first-century greenhouse effect."

Jeremy Rifkin – Entropy

Contemporary literature is now full of more or less imaginative or apocalyptic references to global climate change and its consequences on the world and its civilizations. Despite the resistance of some large countries, the global community has now accepted global warning, at least in general terms, and has agreed to introduce measures to stop (or at least slow down) the devastating effects of climate change on the Earth's ecosystem.

There is, therefore, no need to add much more to the descriptions offered over the years on the subject or to highlight the importance of a paradigm shift in land use and consumption. There is, however, space for thinking that is still profound and sufficiently wide-ranging concerning the way in which architecture (and in particular the design of cities) can interact with on-going climate processes. However, the topic must be segmented into "scales." The "macro" scale of urban and regional planning aims to trace the major strategic orientations for the development of metropolises by working on a number of aspects. The economy, society, transportation, industry, and energy are all matters of paramount importance but they do not say anything to us about the smaller scale "fine grain" of cities. At the other extreme, technology and the construction industry are experimenting with innovative solutions for saving energy in buildings, for reducing costs of the thermoregulation of homes, and limiting the ecological footprint of the materials used. At the heart of the question is a dynamic and mostly unexplored space in which urban form and architecture largely determine the quality of urban life from a climatic point of view and contribute significantly to overall ecological performance. Unfortunately, government attention is meaningfully oriented toward the two extremes of the issue while the options that include the design of the built environment seem less debated. Of course, I do not refer to single virtuous cases but rather to massive and systematic urban planning for new construction according to principles of modern microclimatology.

In policies regarding the effects of energy and climate control on the built heritage, it is necessary to move from a conception of the city as a sum of single buildings to one that corresponds more to its formal and typological characteristics. The scientific literature has primarily proven the effects of urban design on the dynamics of fluids and thus on how the temperature is distributed and humidity is a function of ventilation, just as the awareness of the role of solar orientation is well-established in evaluating the environmental quality of the city. While not lacking the theoretical and technical bases for a shift in scale, it still seems far from being achieved especially in those contexts where the consolidated fabric of the historic city does not allow, except to a very small degree, those reforming large-scale interventions like those undertaken the second half of the nineteenth century in relation to the issue of urban hygiene.

Although the relationship between urban form and climate has been confirmed by the foremost international organizations (ONU, European Commission, etc.) that indicated urban design as one of the preferred tools for creating the future 'sustainable city', today real actions are still very few. The reason for this difficulty can also be attributed to the meaning of 'sustainability' itself and the way it has been pursued in practice. Today, the prevailing approach is a holistic one that views the city as an ecosystem interrelated with its environment.

According to a metabolic approach, urban metabolism is achieved by reaching a perfect balance between energy input and output. It is a necessary condition for labeling a city "sustainable." Even the use of renewable sources can contribute to creating

the required balance; nevertheless, it must be accompanied by an appropriate energy consumption policy. The current strategy is based on the large-scale use of renewable energy sources in buildings and massive use of technology. This approach, the current mainstream, has several drawbacks.

1. The city (as well as the mega-cities of several million inhabitants) is not a stand-alone system; in other words, it is not isolated, so that each process influences the whole planet. It means that city X can obtain a perfect balance for itself through a large use of technology, nevertheless the overall costs of production, transportation, and maintenance of that solution is usually not responsible for the balance of that city or of that nation;

2. The brutal use of technology to provide cities with low-cost "green" energy is radically changing the face of the city. Roofs, facades, walls, and roads change their configuration to adapt to the new devices. Sometimes this is a big issue;

3. The amount of green areas has become a kind of unit for measuring urban quality, a powerful weapon to control carbon dioxide emissions and sometimes just a fashionable way to make an iconic building. Urban parks and garden design, as codified in the past, have been transformed into must-have companions to development;

4. The model does not take in account the planner's mistakes in urban design, whose costs in term of energy consumption and comfort affect the city and must be counterbalanced over time by use of technologies with massive consequences on global energy consumption.

Thus, even if the metabolic approach has focused attention on the macro and micro scales, it does not take into account the intermediate one; in other words, it does not consider the morphology of urban form and its relation to climate on the ground level. Following the rude awakening from the incorrect belief in hydrocarbon's limitless availability, current policy is mainly geared toward increasing efficiency of buildings; nevertheless, this point does not affect urban form.

Good morphology of the urban fabric and the appropriate proportion of blocks dramatically reduce the need for extensive use of hi-technology in construction and its related costs. In fact, current research on the microclimatic behavior of urban space clarifies the actual role of morphology both on energy balance and outdoor/indoor comfort, (see the writings of B. Givoni-2003). Furthermore, several studies have also demonstrated that the benefits of applying energy savings policies to the sum of the single buildings tend to level off.

According to these studies, the possibility of decreasing consumption through singular undertakings will lose their effectiveness on the individual building in the long term, requiring a necessary change in scale of the size of the city (De Pascali, 2008). Consequently, the role and potential of the city in achieving these objectives is also gaining importance in the contemporary international debate. Because of the apparent limitations of the "relative eco-efficiency of the object" (Orlandi), the issue requires a shift toward the urban scale, intended as a set of buildings and open spaces and their mutual physical and topographic relations that regularly interact with climate. Thus, at a time when the world is still looking for a way to preserve its energy sources or is still in transition toward new alternative sources, reducing costs of energy consumption and quality of space, resulting from lack of attention to microclimatic behaviour in design, is dramatically crucial for everyday life.

Rethinking the urban design process in function of 'physical' and environmental parameters, which affect urban energy behaviour, can dramatically increase the energy efficiency of the entire system. If urban energy balance is profoundly influenced by spatial configurations resulting from the very first typo-morphological choices, then managing environmental data during the early stages of the design process can set the right perspective for the design right at the beginning. The microclimatological urban design (MCUD) approach proposed in these notes does not criticize the metabolic approach in itself but rather seeks to highlight the importance of focusing on the intermediate scale. Starting from an MCUD approach, architecture can deploy its total potential through the control of physical parameters of urban form that can interact with climatic phenomena. Many international studies are aimed at defining physical parameters upon which to act to improve the overall performance of space. In the conceptual framework regarding the deep relationship between urban morphology and microclimatic performance, much research has identified some macro-classes of physical parameters like urban density, H\W ratio, settlement form and size, orientation, etc. which are also-urban design parameters. Even if those classes of data are usually considered by engineers to be 'geometric' parameters that can affect the climate on the micro-scale, for urban designers they represent the material with which they work to shape the image of the city. Thus, placing urban design at the core of the sustainability debate prevents the risk of moving too brutally toward a deterministic approach. The required balance between energy savings and architectural and urban needs should be achieved by moving toward an integrated approach.

Today technology lets us forecast not only the weather meticulously but also the interaction between climate and urban form. Computers and advanced software can simulate the effect of the wind on buildings

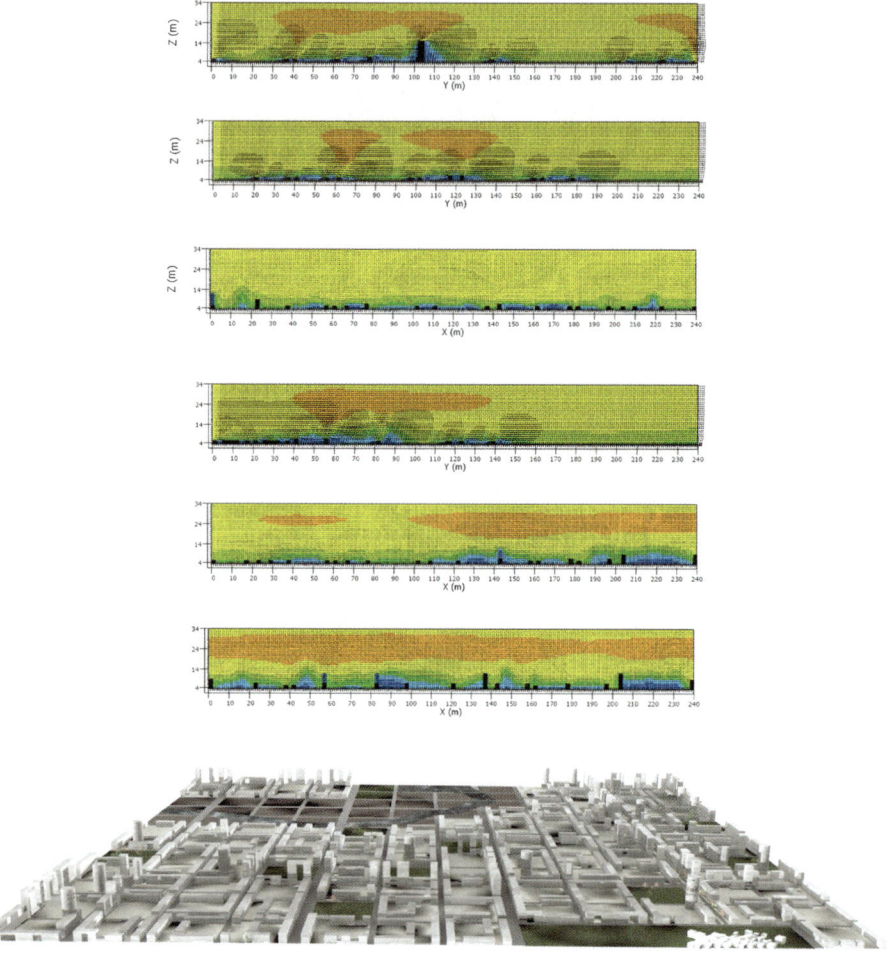

Zhaoqing masterplan

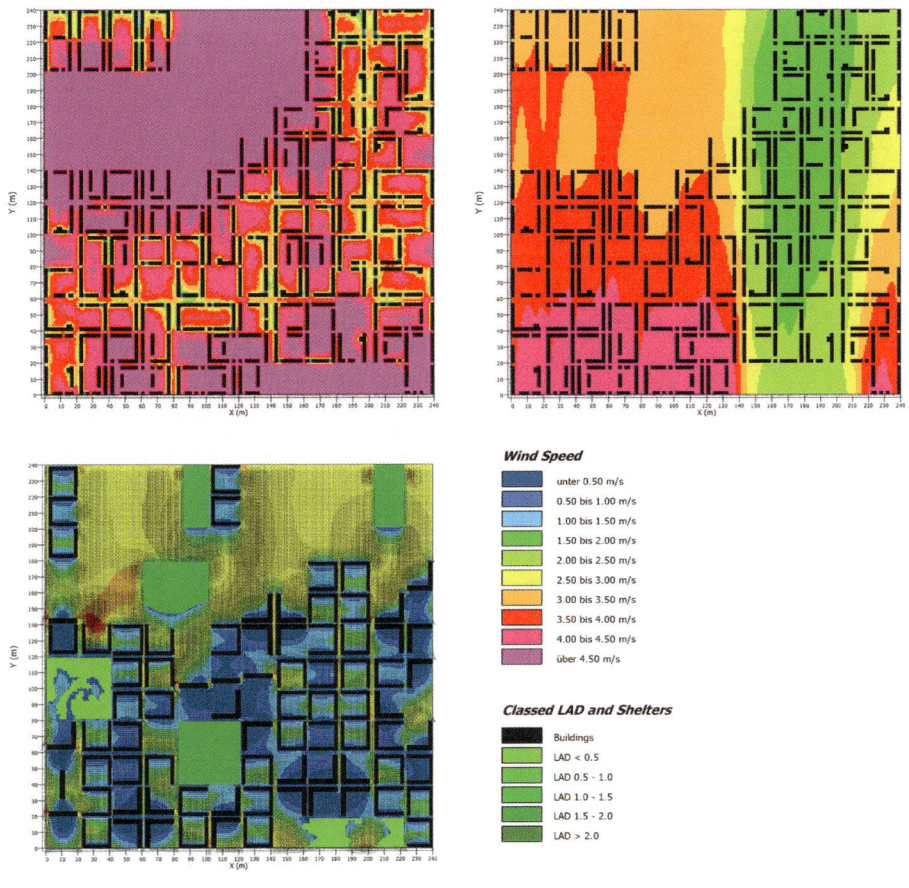

Zhaoqing masterplan - climate simulations

but also on streets, courtyards, squares, and parks. Buildings and public space can be optimized to reach the perfect balance between energy consumption, comfort, and spatial quality. Even if this method is not widely applied in planning today, it is not new to urban design. The most important civilization on the planet has tried to expand its ability to forecast the weather not only to improve agriculture but also to preserve cities and settlements from disaster. Weather is also a powerful weapon on the battlefield. Generals gained the ability to use weather against their enemies to obtain their defeat or retreat due to environmental conditions. But meanwhile, architects and planners were able to draw some advantages from climate to improve the quality and safety of human settlements. Nevertheless, in the past, this kind of control was weak, due to the lack of proper technology. Furthermore, the re-reading of urban history can help us confirm a one-to-one relation between spatial configuration and microclimatic performance or between urban design and energy balance. The form of urban settlements in the Roman Empire was strongly influenced not only by the treatise of Vitruvio but also by the need to optimize the climatic 'efficiency' of the urban fabric. It demonstrates that the topic is not new, but it needs comprehensive study to be fully effective within the theoretical debate around urban design. In the following pages, we also discuss early attempts to organize a new discipline around microclimatic urban design. The contribution that the early pioneers made to the topic remain strong, but the will to establish a comprehensive approach linking architecture, planning, climatology and fluid dynamics still sounds futuristic and ambitious to us even today. This book does want to be a treatise on the topic; rather it opens a field of discussion and offers an opportunity to connect scholars from different fields of knowledge. Sometimes the text will appear overly technical, sometimes less, but in the end, the topic of MCUD will return to the stage providing architects and planners with the opportunity to contribute to solving the risks of our era.

This research project is primarily of a methodological nature and therefore does intend to have a direct impact on current urban design strategies; it is conceived to expand knowledge on advanced urban and architectural design tools, working on theoretical models as well as their experimental implementation through toolkits. The proposed approach is not intended to be the ultimate one, but can hopefully contribute to moving the focus of the current debate on the city to the microclimatic effects of urban form. This innovative point of view offers architects and politicians as well as administrators and competition juries increased awareness of the complicated relationships among climate, comfort, energy consumption and urban form. The primary application of the results will be in fields such as urban and architectural design; it will focus on education, starting from the consideration that the climatic aspects of a project need to be more thoroughly integrated into design teaching in architecture schools.

"Visualize the future impact of all actions (undertaken or not)"

Zygmunt Baumann

CHAPTER TWO

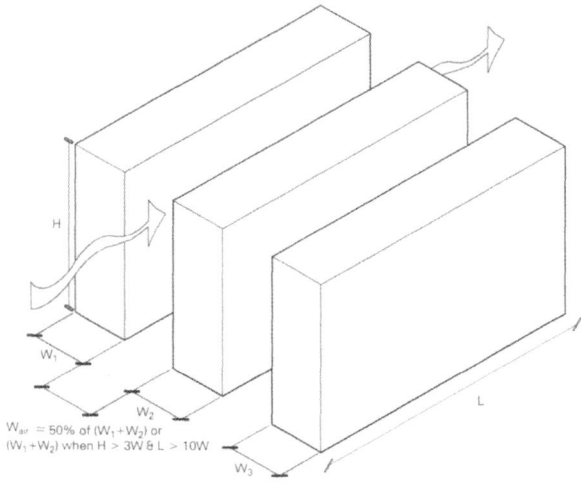

Urban canyon - H\W ratio

Chapter TWO

Key concepts

From the 1970s-80s on, the relationships between urban morphology and local microclimate have been widely tackled in the international scientific debate (Givoni, Olgyvay, Oke, Owens, etc.). Many studies have demonstrated that the formal characteristics of urban settlements strongly affect the performance of the key environmental parameters (wind speed and direction, temperature, humidity, solar radiation, etc.), thus simultaneously determining climatic features on the micro-scale and thermal comfort conditions of a given space. The consequences are not limited to the quality and liveability of a space, according to the degree of well being, but affect the overall energy balance of a city and its needs. In fact, it has been widely demonstrated that the relationships between morphological (orientation, geometry, aspect ratio, sky view factor, etc.) and environmental parameters within the urban fabric determine the intensity with which certain microclimatic phenomena occur. For instance, the "heat-island" effect or the heat trap has significant implications for the energy needs of HVAC systems. The importance of urban morphology concerning human physical and psychological well being was present in the history of architecture in the work and research of prominent figures like L. Hilberseimer and W. Gropius. Their studies for new urban areas measured design choices with the local geographic and climatic conditions, paying great attention to the sun path in different seasons and the distance between fronts (H/W ratio) with the intention of identifying a 'congruous dimension' of the built context that could simultaneously contain "the indiscriminate exploitation of the land" and ensure the proper penetration of air and the sun.

The evolution of the studies and tools available today once again reaffirm the importance of microclimatic control in the early stages of design as a means of ensuring the comfort and quality of a future space, where the term 'quality' defines the correspondence of microclimatic performance of a model with requirements of environmental comfort. This process of control can take place today thanks to the support of important tools that can assist a designer. In fact constant software development makes it possible to work on different scales (urban or architectural), with a necessary simplification and limitation of the study area due to the large quantity and complexity of data and information of real situations. For this reason, applications on the urban scale can mainly return qualitative trends in microclimatic parameters.

This analysis, while departing from a quantitative-prescriptive logic applied to a single building, is valuable in understanding the energy, climatic and environmental impacts of design choices, comparing them with different solutions.

Therefore, this work continues recent international research on the microclimate and energy consequences of urban form. It has some goals that can be summarized in the definition of a scientific method by which the microclimatic behaviours of different design solutions are verified and monitored, bringing design closer to a site by reintroducing topological and climatic features into the design variables.

The optimization of a protocol (or at least a method) for evaluating and comparing the microclimatic behaviour of different urban configurations in order to understand their effect on environmental performance involves the identification of a flexible procedure that can be repeated and adapted to many different situations and, on the other hand, can guarantee the validity of the assessment of the results. Moreover, the introduction of a monitoring system of the overall performance of the project in the early stages of the design allows the designer to act upstream and downstream of the process, reducing the costs (especially energy costs) that are strongly linked to environmental discomfort and the inefficient functioning of the urban organism.

Nevertheless by slowly overcoming the 'mechanistic' view of the city, understood as a sum of independent parts, that has dominated planning until today, we can now make room for a more holistic point of view that conceives the city as an ecosystem strongly tied to place.

According to studies by M. Santamouris (2001), the urban energy balance equation clearly expresses the relationship between urban form and energy performance. Even as a design's aggregate choices define the settlement's physical structure, they also determine the incoming (Q_r) and outgoing ($Q_e + Q_l$) energy flow exchanges, influencing the city's energy–environmental behaviour.

$$[Q_r + Q_t = Q_e + Q_l + Q_s + Q_a]$$

Studies conducted since the 1980s demonstrate the significant role played by urban form in the city's efficient functioning. Research carried out by T.R. Oke (1982), in particular, on the interactions between urban settlements and their environments demonstrate how the typology of the urban fabric affects the intensity with which the urban heat island phenomenon occurs in a city centre.

UHI measures the increase in temperature in central areas of a city resulting from a vicious cycle. In this process, increased temperature has tremendous impacts on building energy consumption due to the

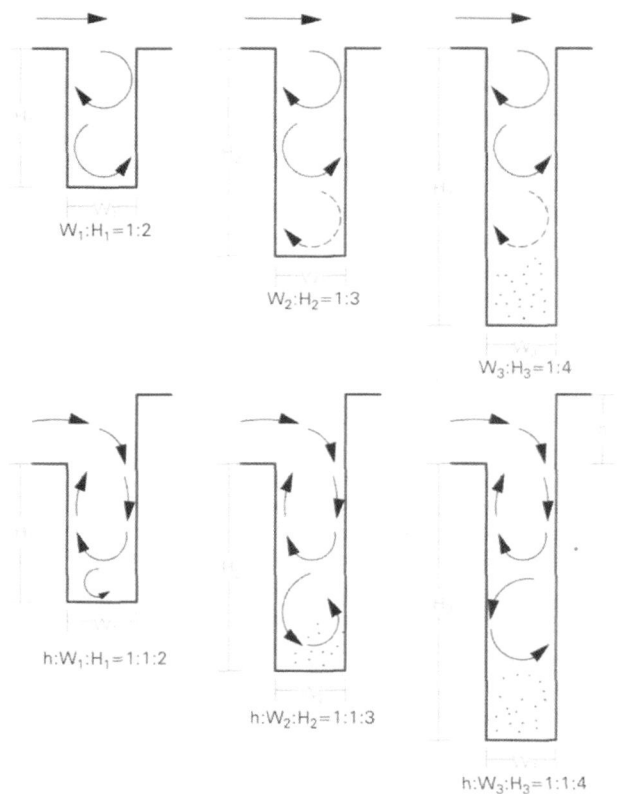

Urban canyon - H\W ratio

growth in energy demand for HVAC systems, thus increasing the release of hot air and other emissions. The Athens case study, conducted by M. Santamouris, demonstrates that the temperature in the city centre can reach a difference of 10°C with respect to surrounding areas, since the requirements for electricity for cooling are three times higher. Several studies performed in the USA (NASA and L.B.L.) (Santamouris, 2001) have studied urban temperature trends in several American cities. For example, the Los Angeles case study revealed a temperature gap of 0.8 F during the last decade with a difference in cooling degree days equal to a 92% increase (1941-1970).

Among the physical parameters affecting the weather–environmental behaviour of urban settlements, scholars have identified the most important value as the height and width ratio (H/W) of building façades (H= building height; W= façade width).

Aside from temperature variations, the H/W ratio is also responsible for the penetration of airflows and solar radiation into the urban fabric. This formal aspect affects a settlement's ability to use natural light and ventilation for indoor and outdoor spaces. In terms of natural ventilation in urban areas, in addition to building geometries, the orientation of the urban fabric with respect to the prevailing winds is quite important. In an urban fabric perpendicular to wind direction, graphs produced by E. Ng show how increases in the H/W ratio correspond to drastically reduced air penetration into the urban canyons. Once the proportion reaches the value of 2:1, wind speed at ground level is close to zero. On the other hand, when the fabric is parallel to wind flow, increased penetration is a function both of façade width and distance (the width between buildings in the urban canyon). According to these studies, values below certain parameters affect urban energy balance, especially regarding air temperature differences in the city centre, wind speed variation in the urban canyons, and the rate of solar radiation on the ground level. Thus, the aspect ratio is directly related to the intensity of the 'urban heat island' (UHI) and consequently work on physical, geometric and typological factors indirectly affects the energy balance of a city and its overall efficiency.

The main consequences of the aspect ratio on the climatic/environmental performance of the settlements can be summarized as follows:

- H/W and the urban airflow

The "jaggedness" of an urban settlement influences wind flow within the urban canyon. According to Oke, building geometry obstructs natural air movement, defining two different layers located above and below roof level (boundary layer; urban canopy layer). Within the urban canopy layer, the relationship between urban geometry and wind direction impacts average wind speed and, consequently, the natural ventilation of the urban fabric. The orientation of the urban grid with regard to the prevailing wind direction and urban geometry identifies various wind regimes.

When the canyon axis is perpendicular to air flow, secondary flow at ground level relates strictly to the aspect ratio, so that it will be reduced at greater values (> 0.65). «Naturally, this condition provides greater shelter to pedestrians from undesirable wind, but at other times may impede necessary ventilation of the urban space» (Erell, Pearlmutter, Williamson, 2011).

On the contrary, when the axis of the urban grid is parallel to wind flow, secondary airflow circulation is a function both of width and façade distance. According to E. Neg: «For the air path to be effective, the width of the air path at the windward side should be at least, and on average, 50 per cent of the total widths of the buildings on both sides. The width needs to be increased when the heights of the buildings increase» (Ng, 2010).

• H/W and solar radiation access
Regarding solar radiation access within the urban canyons, in addition to the H/W ratio, settlement location plays a prominent role in controlling daylight and sunlight. On the one hand, greater distance between building façades fosters natural lighting of indoor and outdoor spaces and improves building health and human psychophysical well being. On the other hand, in hot regions, greater distance can contribute to overheating of building surfaces, increasing indoor and outdoor air temperatures.

Research developed by A. Tsangrassoulis in 2001 (Santamouris, 2001) concerning the need to deploy natural lighting linked urban geometries to latitude. The results suggested that designers should decrease H/W ratio in relation to increases in latitude, a practice already well established in "good construction techniques".

Specifically, Tsangrassoulis identifies three optimal H/W ratio values with relation to three different latitudes: 40° (H\W=0.7) 45° (H\W=0.58) 50° (H\W=0.46)

The study of the microclimatic interactions between urban form and local climatic/environmental conditions took into consideration seven main parameters divided into two classes:

• Morphological: aspect ratio (H/W), orientation and sky view factor (SVF);
• Environmental: temperature (°C), relative humidity (%), wind speed (m/s) and direction (deg°), direct solar radiation (kWh/m^2)

The environmental parameters must be considered as site information; they generally correspond to the more critical days of the year. The morphological parameters, especially the H\W factor, depend both on design choices and the need for microclimatic optimization; thus a balance can be achieved as a result of an iterative process. With this key concept, the urban designer can optimize a preliminary layout step-by-step by applying a methodological approach summarized in the following points:

1. Design of a preliminary design proposal;
2. Microclimatic analysis of spatial configurations, taking into consideration the climatic conditions of the site in order to identify the main critical conditions;
3. Modification of the initial design to improve the critical factors identified;
4. Microclimatic verification of the new improved contributions;
5. Definition of a final design solution deemed sufficient.

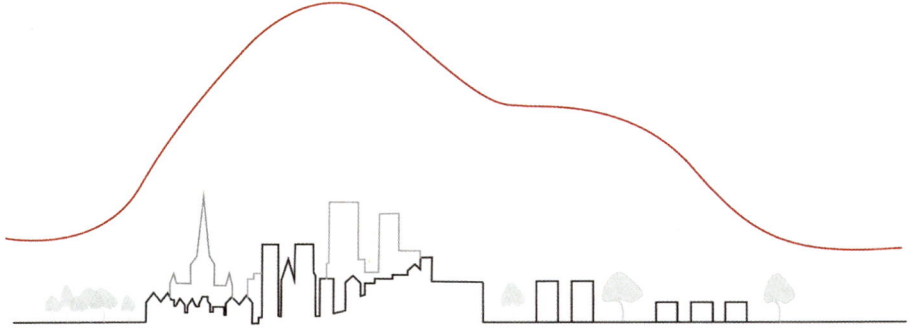

Boundary layer

"Ut flatus aurae aestus exercitus leniat."

Hyginius Gromaticus

CHAPTER THREE

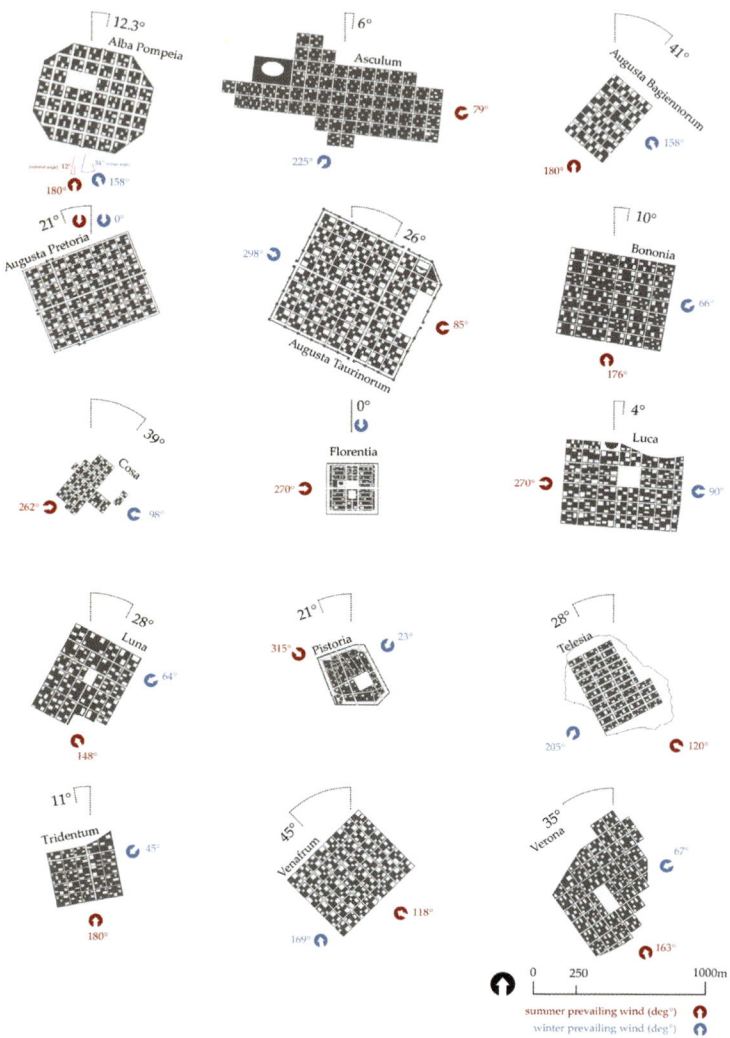

Orientation of some Roman cities in relation to the prevailing wind

Chapter THREE

Genealogy

This chapter focuses on a topic that has already been discussed and published; nevertheless the need to trace a sort of genealogy is still strategic. In order to demonstrate that, even if the term urban sustainability might be relatively new, the issue is not; the aforementioned publication sought to demonstrate the ability of ancient Roman engineers to plan new settlements by optimizing local climatic conditions. This approach can be easily considered a sort of proto-urban microclimatology. Even if is not the purpose of this book to provide in-depth historic research on Roman urban settlements, this chapter explores the approach of ancient civilizations to urban design in the very early steps of the process from a climate perspective. The Roman approach is not applicable today; nevertheless it highlights the importance of a holistic approach that has been neglected in more current times.

One of the authors who wrote about the topic in 1935was the unknown Italian architect Gaetano Vinaccia. He was a pioneer of urban microclimatology during the 1930s–1940s, and he was probably the first to focus attention on the environmental features of the Roman foundation process, correlating urban grid orientation with annual sun path and wind direction. Even if Vinaccia is considered a minor figure in the architectural literature, his studies on the relationship between urban form and local microclimate can be considered innovative for the time. Vinaccia's approach was mainly based on his attempt to extend microclimatic issues to the urban scale (Polis-climatology). Today when current global energy and environmental conditions compel professionals to rethink design and planning processes concerning energy containment and the improvement of human comfort, his lessons appear to be extremely effective in the development of 'environmental design,' especially concerning the urban scale. The following chapter will offer some information on this figure and the role he played in scientific history. Here we focus on one of his most important publications, "Il Problema dell'Orientamento nell'Urbanistica dell'Antica Roma" (1935). The author's theories were based on ancient manuscripts, particularly Vitruvius who stated that: «[cities] will be well built if winds are wisely kept out from squares and streets; [winds] which offended if cold, vitiate if hot, harm if wet.» The ancient knowledge of winds was manifested in the construction of a bronze wind rose, representing a triton, on which the 12 prevailing winds were depicted; Flavius Eutropius probably built the station during the empire of

37

Valentinian II. According to the mythological representation of the winds, 'annoying' winds came from north/north-westerly directions (cold winds), whereas 'unhealthy' winds arrived from the south/south-east (usually, hot wet winds)

In the manuscript, the author affirmed Roman planning ability, highlighting the fact that the design process also included the environmental features of a site. The theory of Vinaccia was based on the close relationship between the orientation of Roman new cities and local environmental conditions, especially concerning winds. According to Vinaccia, the Roman grid was oriented to take into account the main directions of the 'annoying' winds (cold) and the 'unhealthy' (hot-humid) ones to avoid their penetration into urban space.

Ancient manuscripts, such as Vitruvius's "De Architectura" and Hyginius Gromaticus's "De Castris Romanis", contain some evidence of Vinaccia's theory; nevertheless the statements on Roman technical ability in combining wind protection issues with those related to urban foundation strategies (such as military, political) were never confirmed until today. Current technology like Computational Fluid Dynamics (CFD) software offers us the opportunity to overcome the lack of validation of Vinaccia's work; applying a CFD approach to the same cases in Vinaccia's work gives us the opportunity to confirm his results. The study was carried out on 15 Italian Roman-founded cities; they were analysed in relation to urban form and the relationship between grid orientation and local wind conditions. The point that we can confirm is that the Roman-founded city or military camp (from which numerous existing cities originated) was driven by considerable attention to local climatic conditions - wind conditions in particular - which were accurately coupled with military, economic and political issues in order to improve urban comfort and reduce health risks. Even if is a widespread belief that the origins of the orientation of the urban grid along the cardinal points were tied to religion, Roman planning was mainly based on a pragmatic approach that concerned both topography and microclimatic aspects strictly relating to local winds and the sun path. It is well known that the Romans adapted a general plan illustrated in manuals to the real character of a site; nevertheless this adaptive approach was driven not only by topographic or military issues but also by climatic needs.

According to Benevolo (Benevolo, 2006), in Roman farmland divisions (centuratio), the orientation of the grid already moved from alignment along the cardinal points to take advantage of the form of the territory. The same approach was also taken in city construction following the precepts of Vitruvius and Hyginus: the grid rotated to follow the best orientation in relation to wind conditions. The orientation of the grid was part of a design strategy to improve urban hygiene and climatic comfort throughout the year. The Romans' great attention to local airflow conditions basically tends to avoid the penetration of 'annoying' (cold) and 'unhealthy' (hot-humid) winds into urban spaces. The study of more than 60 examples of Roman castra in military camps in Italy, Britain, France, and Germany by Gaetano Vinaccia address the evidence of a degree of deviation of the Cardo Maximus (the central north-south oriented axis) from the north. It highlighted the absence of a direct relationship with cardinal points and points out the relationship between the orientation of the urban fabric (based on the intersection of orthogonal axes: cardus—generally in a north-south direction, and decumanus—east-west direction) and the prevailing wind. Vinaccia's study of Roman military camps in Britannia took into account eleven cases: Gellycaer, Temple Brogh, Brecon Gaer, Castel Collen, Slack, Carnavon (Segontium), Cardiff, Eslack, Brogh-by-Bainbridge, Cappuck, Bar Hill. The author mapped out the general plan of each camp and indicated its orientation, the main wind direction and the angle of deviation of wind direction from the central camp axis. The overall orientation data and castra plans are included in the Vinaccia text (Vinaccia, 1939). His study introduced concepts regarding the relationship between grid orientation and sun pattern and touched the importance of sunlight in the passive heating of buildings. Nevertheless, his research mainly concerned wind conditions and Italian cities. With the purpose of essentially discovering a general rule (which would have been re-used for Italian colonies) Vinaccia tried to identify a constant value in grid rotation; however, he was always perfectly aware of local differences in wind direction and velocity, which could have suggested different grid orientations for each city. Vinaccia estimated this value to be about 22.3° east. This angle, which coincides with a quarter of a quadrant, should allow each settlement, through its form, to contrast the penetration of cold winds from north and north-west and hot-humid winds from the south and south-east directions respectively into the urban grid.

"Intra murum arearum divisiones platearumque et angiportum ad caeli regionem directiones. Dirigentur haec autem recte, si exclusi erunt ex angiportis venti prudenter. Qui si frigidi sunt, laedunt; si calidi, vitiant; si umidi, nocent"
[the inner area is divided, and streets and squares function according to sky regions. These will be built correctly if the wind is excluded from the streets because if these [winds, ed.] are cold, they will damage; if hot, they will taint; if humid, they will harm] (Vitruvio, De Architectura, Caption 6).

Once a site's fitness was determined and exterior walls built, the city foundation process was precisely described by Vitruvius.

In his main text, De Architectura, Vitruvius reveals his in-depth knowledge of wind and its classification and characteristics. His knowledge was based on ancient Greek studies, which were the first on the topic (Passe & Battaglia, 2015). The first octagonal wind tower in Athens built by Andronikos di Kiyrrhos during the first and second centuries B.C. was able to indicate the direction and features of flowing wind through a bronze Triton placed on top of the tower. The Triton was free to move; it pointed toward one of the eight sides of the tower where the correspondent wind personification was depicted, highlighting its personality and character. Vitruvius also proposed a city sheltered from the wind; however, we must consider that, in ancient times, knowledge of wind directions and their features was essential for various other activities, including navigation and farming. Naturally these activities transcend urban microclimate and human comfort. Vegezio and Hyginus Gromaticus in "De Castris Romanorum" also introduced some suggestions for the castrum plan organization concerning wind protection. Hyginus analysed street dimensions and row arrangements of military camps "Castra [...] tertiata esse debebunt ut flatus aurae aestus exercitus leniat" (The camp should be divided into three parts, so that airflow can relieve the heat of the army.) The relationship between urban form and microclimatic conditions emerges in ancient texts even if contemporary researchers rarely mention Roman planning. While the modifications imposed by local terrain had been addressed in Zanker (2013), Sommella (1988) and Benevolo (2006), surprisingly there is no trace of a complete analysis in Vitruvius, Vegezio, and Hyginus. In 1993, Benevolo emphasized the Greek origins of Roman orthogonal urban plans, descending from Hippodamus of Miletus, but omitting its relation to local climate. Evidence of the environmental effects of the orientation and dimensions of the Greek grid in relation to sun access and wind penetration was explored by Butti and Perlin (1980), as well as Castagnoli (1956) who pointed out that Hyppodamus was also called "meteorologist". In their exploration of urban morphology, Caniggia e Maffei (2002) analysed the shape, geometry and orientation of ancient military settlements but omitted orientation and local climate.

In 2004, Conventi recovered Vitruvius's heritage in a certain sense, stating that deviation of the grid from the north was a common Roman approach aimed at improving winter sunlight and wind protection. The study examined 40 Italian cases. The author observed a general propensity toward an eastward deviation off the north-south urban axis (Cardo Maximus) confirming Vinaccia's affirmations, without, however, mentioning his studies.

Conventi's work appears to be the most complete on this topic, and his approach is close to Vinaccia's. Unfortunately, even if the thinking of the Italian architect resembles the more updated contemporary research, he is considered a minor figure both in national and international architectural reviews. His work can be considered the first attempt to connect climatology to urban design with the aim of founding a new discipline that he called "polis-climatology."

The purpose of the study that we published in 2017 was to verify Vinaccia's hypotheses regarding the relationship between Roman grid orientation and wind protection. However, this research is more extensive. The confirmation of the hypothesis proposed by Vinaccia could place him among the founders of a new discipline that is so current and important today. The opportunity to consider the Italian architect as a pioneer in urban microclimatology can establish a sort of genealogy for future scholars who would like to delve into this topic more deeply.

With today's environmental conditions, researchers worldwide rethink the paradigms of future urban development by redesigning the planning process from its basis. "Environmental design" is currently most effective way to resolve urban sustainability. Nevertheless, the unique ability of some pioneers like the ancient Romans and modern architects such as Vinaccia provide excellent lessons on how to couple different theories and laws from outside disciplines (physics, chemistry, medicine, etc.) with architectural fundamentals, thus underscoring the astonishing modernity of their thought.

The study was divided into three main phases, developed in the same way for each case: data collection, morphological analyses and three-dimensional reconstruction of Roman urban plans; identification of local weather data was the intermediate step; and analysis of urban ventilation using CFD software was the last and more technical part.

The work focused on 15 Italian Roman cities: Alba Pompeia (Alba, province of Cuneo), Asculum (Ascoli Piceno), Augusta Bagiennorum (Bene Vagienna, province of Cuneo), Augusta Praetoria (Aosta), Augusta Taurinorum (Turin), Bononia (Bologna), Cosa (Ansedonia, province of Grosseto), Florentia (Florence), Luca (Lucca), Luna (Luni, province of La Spezia), Pistoria (Pistoia), Telesia (Telese Terme, province of Benevento), Tridentum (Trento), Venafrum (Venafro, province of Isernia) and Verona (Verona). The list of cases was determined by the availability of reliable data concerning both the urban geometries of the Roman nucleus and climatic data. To collect the necessary data we referred to a number of resources. Most studies on Roman cities show some traces of the original urban plan. Frequently the original plan has been lost due to their transformations over time. According to Conventi, in fact: "the perimeter of urban walls is considered an essential part of the topographic reconstruction of centres. From the correct delineation of the urban circuit [...] depends the exact grid planning" (Conventi, 2004). Data used in this study were mainly obtained from Conventi's datasheet and integrated with additional prior references. To understand the original approach to planning in each case, the study collected information concerning data of the foundations, local political statutes (Roman colony, Latin colony, Municipium, etc.), geographic coordinates and topographic conditions (flatlands, hills, slopes, and plateaus). This data was considered to be the main factors that could have influenced urban form. Concerning morphological data relating to urban structure, the study focused on general dimensions (exterior perimeters, streets, and blocks), number of blocks (insulae) and grid orientation. The last was crucial for the study. In fact, the cardo maximus's deviation from the north was measured precisely just as Vinaccia had previously done.

Each case study was successively modelled both two-dimensionally and three-dimensionally. Plan reproduction matched both existing sketches with data. According to scholars (Maffei, 2002) (Conventi, 2004), the insulae (blocks), which were located in the central part of the city, were mainly constituted by the domus. The Roman " domus " has been recognized by Maffei (2002) as the principal Roman building typology, which was used during the transformation of a military camp into a colony. The domus appeared to be linked to more prosperous Roman families, who could afford individual villas of about 800-1000 m2. The only well-known examples of Roman urban block layout are in Pompeii, from which it is possible to extrapolate useful information regarding their spatial organization.

To collect information and data on wind conditions primarily relating to the Roman period, this work refers to the current discipline of paleoclimatology. According to some scholars, (Behringer, 2010; Chen, Zonneveld, & Versteegh, 2011; Büntgen et al., 2011; Wang, Surge, & Walker, 2013; McCormick et al., 2012) the Roman Empire had an exceptionally warmer, more stable condition from 60 B.C. to 200. As a result, air temperatures during the Roman period were similar to today's and current climatic data extrapolated from the Meteonorm database can still be considered reliable. Furthermore, average wind direction and intensity have been obtained from the most nearby local weather stations.

The case studies are divided into three groups based on the angle of incidence resulting from wind direction and the city's grid axis upon which it is directed (0–10º; 15–30º; >35º).

Although local environmental conditions characterize each city, it is possible to obtain results from morphological and CFD analyses. The first point is that among the 15 cases, there are five that can be defined as 'special' because of their local orographic and soil context that had previously determined the urban layout. These cases are Augusta Taurinorum, Augusta Pretoria, Luca, Florentia, and Cosa. The impact of the Alps on local climate is dramatic in the first two cases, Augusta Pretoria and Augusta Taurinorum. In fact, their proximity to those high mountains protects them from wind all year round. The grid orientation can thus be considered to be more independent from local wind directions.

Augusta Pretoria is the sixth highest Italian city (583 m a.s.l.) and is characterized by cold winters; nevertheless its location in a valley protects the settlement from seasonal winds, obstructing both cold airflows and fresh summer breezes, causing the opposing problem of humidity. The Western Alps protect Turin (Augusta Taurinorum) from prevailing northwest winter winds, whereas some hills on to east obstruct prevailing summer winds coming from this direction.

Luca and Florentia are different. Both cities are wet, which profoundly influenced their form. The place-name, Luca, according to Barracchini (1997), probably relates to the ancient Ligurian 'luk' that means 'marshy land'; Florentia's might originate from the ancient Etruscan 'Birenz' (among the waters, Maffei 2002). Both cities are perfectly positioned along the north-south axis, allowing winter and summer airflows to penetrate deeply into the urban fabric, removing natural humidity. The last 'special case' is Cosa, which can be understood as a specific solution to a precise environmental condition. The city was located on a promontory extending into the Tyrrhenian Sea at 114 m a.s.l. on the side of the Argentario Mountain in Tuscany to dominate both maritime and land traffic. The exposure of the settlement to the prevailing local winds forced Romans to over-rotate the grid of 41° east to counter pose the urban fabric to prevailing winds, protecting inner urban space from bothersome conditions.

The remaining 10 cases clearly show different seasonal behaviours. According to F. Allard (Allard, Ghiaus, & Szucs, 2009), to improve urban ventilation in dense cities, it is better to limit street deviation from prevailing winds to less than 30°; conversely for values greater than 30° air penetration can be reduced dramatically. It confirms that to improve natural airflow in the summer, a deviation of 30° or less of the urban fabric axis from the seasonal wind is strictly required. On the contrary, for protection

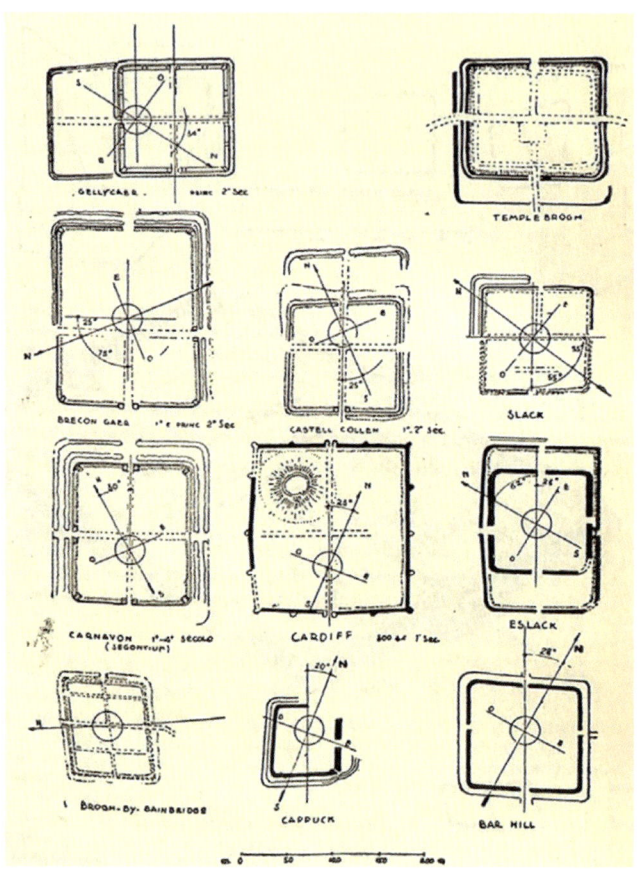

Orientation of Roman cities. From Gaetano Vinaccia

from the winter winds, significant airflow obstruction is preferable; this can be granted by a rotation of 45° (+\- 10°) from the face of wind exposure. In eight cases out of 10, Venafrum, Bononia, Luna, Alba Pomepia, Teleia, Asculum, Tridentum and Pistoria had deviations of their grid axes from the main winter wind direction in the range of 34–54° (an average angle 44°); five out of 10 cases (Tridentum, Asculum, Alba Pompeia, Bononia and Venafrum) revealed a summer angle of less than 20° fostering greater ability to use natural ventilation during the hottest period. This dual capacity can be better understood by taking into account the specific environmental features of each case.

Tridentum is located at 194 m a.s.l., and it is surrounded by high mountains (between 1000 and 2000 m a.s.l.). Winter is unusually frigid with heavy snowfalls. Conversely, during the summer the same mountains can produce wet conditions. In fact, humidity is partially mitigated by an urban orientation limited to 11° from the direction of the principal summer winds.

Asculum is characterized by a sub-Apennine climate with a cold, humid winter. Balkan streams together with the 'Stau' effect produce frequent, strong snowfalls and low temperatures with late frosts and fog. During the summer, the city suffers the heat, which is alleviated by fresh breezes.

Alba Pompeia is characterized by a typical Po valley climate: cold winters and hot, humid summers. It requires ventilation to mitigate dampness and humidity.

Bononia is described as 'a site rich in waters' (Maffei, 2002); the settlement exploits its orientation to fight the cold winters, a product of the nearby Tuscan-Emilian Apennines, and the very hot-humid summers, which require greater airflow.

Venafrum is sited on a slope near the Santa Croce Mountain (1026 m a.s.l.). Its orientation protects it from the northwest and southeast cold waves, at the same mitigating time the hot and humid summer conditions.

Pistoria, Telesia, and Luna show explicit protection of the settlements during the cold season. Pistoria is, in fact, recognized as one of the coldest Tuscan cities where humidity amplifies the sensation of cold. Luna, located in the Gulf of La Spezia, is designed to oppose the conditions influenced mainly by the sea. Verona and Augusta Baggianorum are the only two cases that did not show clear seasonal tendencies. In the case of Verona, its urban organization is sufficiently favourable to the local wind, and can probably be read in terms of a local microclimate characterized by much fog and moisture.

Numerical values of seasonal wind intensity obtained from CFD simulations support the previous considerations. Such values were generated in correspondence to specific 'control points' and subsequently used to estimate an average value, in percentage terms, of 'wind downfall' in relation to wind entrance measured right at the edge of the urban area. Downfall percentages show increasing values corresponding to increasing incidence angles, resulting from main wind directions and the grid axis of the city. Results confirmed a seasonal wind reduction of about −30% in the first group of cities (0–10°), −50% for the second (15–30°) and >−60% for the third (>35), supporting the argument of different seasonal behaviours in these cities.

Even if the results did not confirm any of Vinaccia's values - to about 22.3° east- it is possible to point out the great ability of Roman planners in the management of environmental conditions through urban design, which was precisely the aim of Vinaccia's study.

In conclusion, Roman environmental design ability is now crucial historical evidence; it is demonstrated in its coupling of urban health issues with military, economic and political ends during the foundation of a new city (or military camp—castrum).

*

Starting from the pioneers of the past, interdisciplinary professionals of today like architects and engineers now have useful tools and knowledge for understanding the microclimatic consequences of the initial choices relating to urban or architectural form. This new 'environmental consciousness' in urban design could introduce a new method to integrate both environmental data and analyses within the design process. This approach could accompany all phases of the process from the original concept to final design introducing frequent monitoring and evaluation actions regarding the microclimatic effects of built form.

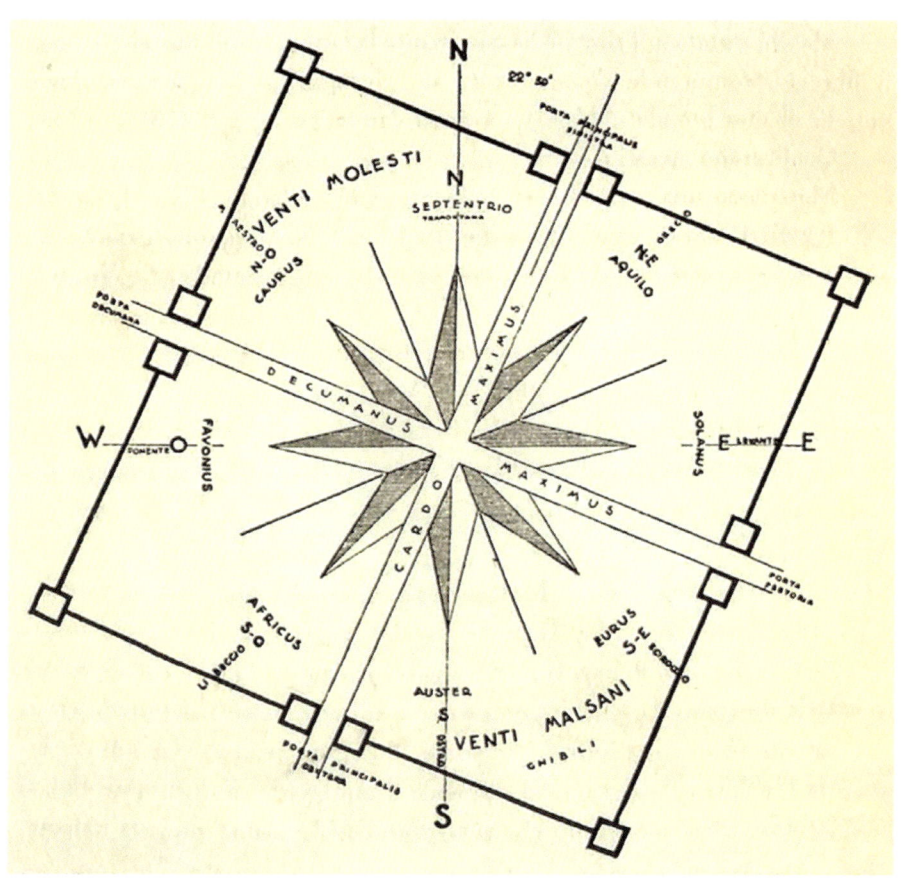

Layout of Roman Castrum. From Gaetano Vinaccia

* Box Extract from
"The environmental elements of foundations in Roman cities: A theory of the architect Gaetano Vinaccia" by Ilaria Giovagnorio, Daniela Usai, Alessandro Palmas, Giovanni Marco Chiri

In order to study wind conditions in the urban area, a virtual wind tunnel was built around each three-dimensional model. The wind tunnel was oriented along the prevailing local summer and winter wind directions. The computational domain, equivalent to the virtual wind tunnel (or building box), was built in order to ensure that each side's width was equal to that of the city (in the case of models of significant dimensions, the domain width was assumed to be equal to half the model width) and that the length was equal to that of the city model in the entry face (before the model), and twice that of the model after it. The domain height corresponds to 35 m, around nine times the building height. The overall dimensions respected Bechmann's recommendations on the best measures in relation to flow simulations (Moonen, Dorer, & Carmeliet, 2011). The computational grid used a tetrahedral grid of variable dimensions, from between 0.5/1 m and 5 m. Additionally, in this case, the choice of the smaller dimension depended on the overall model dimensions and, consequently, on the software's calculation power. For each case study, between five and eight million tetrahedral grids were used. Both the city and the wind tunnel models were imported into the CONSELF® platform (www.conself.com) in order to simulate urban ventilation using CFD software. The software uses a steady Reynolds-averaged Navier–Stokes (RANS) approach with a k- turbulence model. CONSELF® has developed a cloud computing system which allows experts to manage CFD calculations on demand, from the initial modelling phase to the final results. Through the cloud simulations it is possible to use external servers, which allowed us to free up important space on personal computers, otherwise reserved for software installation and execution. Regarding the Boundary Conditions (BCs), calculation were made in the absence of a temperature effect, thus avoiding having to take into account the thermal component. The following conditions for each surface of both the domain and the model were used. Both at the bottom of the building box (on the 'ground') and on the buildings a no-slip wall BCs was imposed, corresponding to flow over smooth surfaces. Three types of lateral boundaries were used on the domain's vertical surfaces. On the inflow boundary, the 'inlet' flow speed (m/s) and the hydraulic diameter (useful for turbulence calculation) were used. A uniform inlet flow, which was modified through the roughness parameter assigned to the ground, was also used. The choice of the appropriate roughness value was made according to Blocken's recommendations on the parameter's correct specifications in an urban context (Blocken, 2015), thus evaluating the mean value based on the surrounding environment for the given wind direction. The atmospheric pressure was imposed on the outlet boundary and a symmetry condition was imposed on the remaining lateral boundary. Finally, an 'inlet velocity vector' condition was assigned to the top of the building box assuming an undisturbed air flow at that height. The model's dimensions influenced both the computational grid, as stated before, and the duration of the simulation, which took a few hours in the smallest cases, and up to 10–12 h for the most complex models. Software validation was developed according to the most contemporary expert guidelines (Moonen, Defraeye, Dorer, Blocken, & Carmeliet, 2012; Oberkampf & Trucano, 2002; Tominaga et al., 2008; Toparlar et al., 2015; Versteeg & Malalasekera, 1995). As suggested by Blocken (2015), since experimental data for the case study were not available, the validation process can be achieved by performing generic sub-configurations contained in high quality experimental online datasets. Results achieved with the CONSELF®software were compared both with wind tunnel datasets, developed by CEDVAL–Hamburg University, and others software results found in scientific literature, for the same sub-configuration. Data processing and visualization were managed using ParaView software. Numerical values, regarding wind intensity, were extracted at a height of 1.5 m in correspondence to specific 'control points'. The locations of the points were chosen to evaluate wind intensity in urban fabrics in order to understand if the influence of grid orientation exists (and to what degree in percentage terms).

"...taking advantage of the fruits of those pioneers who will be considered by them as past-lovers."

Gaetano Vinaccia

CHAPTER **FOUR**

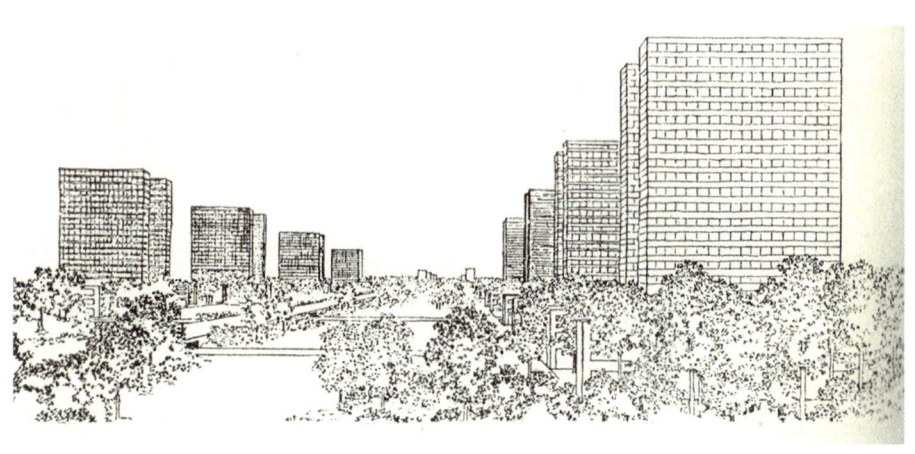

Ludwig Hilberseimer

Chapter FOUR

Pioneers

As illustrated in the previous chapter, the history of environmental design finds its roots in the ancient essays by such Latin authors as Varrone, Columella, Cato, and Vitruvius and in common Roman planning practice that was primarily rediscovered during the Renaissance. L.B. Alberti's urban theories, contained in De Re Aedificatoria, based mainly on Vitruviuan principles, influenced planning in the fifteenth century, pointing out local microclimatic characteristics. According to Benevolo, European colonies in American territories are the most significant urban planning examples from the sixteenth century. New cities employed an urban grid usually defined by square blocks. In 1573, Philip II codified this model into the first town planning act of the modern era. The law included some recommendations for protecting the public square from prevailing winds, confirming the Roman approach described in the previous chapter. No further studies have been completed to demonstrate the application of Vitruvian principles in new colonial towns in south and Central America; nevertheless microclimatic advantages of the older grids, as compared to the successive Jeffersonian one for instance, have been studied by R. Knowles for the city of Los Angeles. The author highlighted the relationship between Spanish grid orientation (nearly 45°) and sea breezes, and the optimal performance of the grid in terms of solar access throughout the year. In Renaissance examples, the bioclimatic approach to building was common. In his essay published in 1570, I Quattro libri dell Architettura (The Four Books of Architecture), one of the most important Renaissance treatises, several essential references concerned both architectural and urban issues. Particularly interesting are Palladio's considerations on villa siting (Chapter XI, Book II) and on urban streets (Chapter II, Book III), where his thinking extends from buildings to the surrounding areas. Concerning the latter, the author suggests orientations and dimensions as functions of solar access and local wind conditions, in strict coherence with Vitruvian recommendations. Despite this vital premise, the topic was neglected until the first half of the twentieth century when just one isolated forerunner sought to integrate some key concepts of microclimatology with urban design and architecture. Even if the terms 'Urban microclimatology' or 'Environmental design' have now become quite common in the current debate, "The City of Tomorrow" (1943-1952) by Gaetano Vinaccia (1881-1971) can be still considered the first complete treatise on the topic.

Vinaccia was unable to participate in the international debate and until today, had no chance of influencing architecture and urbanism. In particular, his impact on rationalist architecture was negligible. Critics have classified Vinaccia as a minor architect, thus any greater study of his scientific production was not possible. Even if he was up to date with the current trends as an architect, his minor role in science and art history is largely due to the fact that he did not belong to a distinct discipline; furthermore his career evolved in quite an unfavourable context. From a current point of view, Gaetano Vinaccia, apart from Latin classics, can be easily considered an "early bird" in that new discipline that he called "polis-climatology", now named "environmental design." A comparison between Vinaccia's content and some contemporary research points out the brilliance of his scientific production. Nevertheless, the cultural environment in which he took his first steps largely characterized by the rise of the so-called Modern Movement and in Italy by the confrontation between traditionalists and rationalists hindered Vinaccia's studies from influencing the international debate.

*

Architects in the early decades of the twentieth century moved the focus of the discipline from a super-structural dimension to the radical reform of the relationship between architecture and society. According to the leading critics, the Modern Movement's first aim was to seek a just society starting from urban planning and building programs. The will to shape an equal society drove the actors of that era to look at goods not only as products to be consumed but rather as social needs to be satisfied. The new architecture not only rewrote the paradigms of the discipline to fit the needs of the working class but also re-thought the basis of the design process itself. In this radical reform, figures like Gropius and Meyer played leading roles in disseminating the spirit of the Neue Sachlichkeit. The Bauhaus provided a new method for the design of objects, furniture, houses, and cities. Architects became more directly involved (as managers and planners) in urban development programs, and the entire design process became more sensitive to social needs, the optimization of form and costs, and material and functional needs.

Even if Friedrich Engels set out the topic of the healthiness of buildings in his 1844 text "The Condition of the Working Class in England" (1844), it was never studied methodically in the research on the 'minimum dwelling' of the Modern Movement.

During CIAM II in Frankfurt (1929), architects like Hannes Meyer, Mart Stam, Walter Gropius, Erns May and Alexander Klein presented their answers to the so-called "Existenzminimum" question. Their proposals sought to reduce building costs (including the cost of land consumption) by reducing the worthless areas in houses, optimizing the building process, repeating typologies, and standardizing construction components. The human being was seen merely as a "biological unit" who requires rest until the following working day so that focus was driven by the very technical and specific issues of the working-class environment. Carlo Aymonino noted that - because all demands for the representation of social status (as well as taste, preferences, and differences) were considered an aspect of bourgeois social life and thus abandoned during the CIAM conference - no one showed images directly describing spatial quality. Presentations described only graphics regarding spatial organization, amounts of daylight, fresh-air flows, strategies for maximizing heat, silence and so on. The next year, focus moved to the city. According to Sigfried Gideon, the third CIAM congress (Brussels, 1930) set the goal of achieving the most effective formulation for buildings on different scales. The leadership of Walter Gropius tried to guide the approach of the early Modern Movement in breaking up the structure of contemporary society. To make it easier to establish a socialist society in Europe, all differences between social classes would have to be eliminated, starting with urban space. The 'mechanical precision' used in the previous CIAM to define new standards in housing was applied to urban design in Brussels. Walter Gropius proposed some long high-rise blocks that were north-south oriented to ensure maximum and equal sun exposure for the apartments. This approach was influenced by the work of the Deutscher Werkbund and in particular by Theodor Fisher (1862-1938), Otto Heasler (1880-1962) and Roman Friedrich Heiligenthal (1880-1951).

Theodor Fisher (1862-1938) was the first chairman of Deutscher Werkbund and professor at the Technical University of Munich; at Alte Heide he realized a plan in which each block is located at a distance equal to twice its height from the others in order to prevent façade shading; this rule was applied five years later by Otto Heasler in the Georgsgarten Siedlung. But this basic rule became the standard for new linear high-rise-blocks based in the neighbourhoods of the Neue Sachlichkeit when R.F. Heiligenthal published his book "Deutsche Städtebau" ("German city planning") in 1921. Gropius' diagrams, shown at CIAM III, were mainly Heiligenthal's, but after his presentation, the Heiligenthal rule achieved a sort of political legitimation. The 1930 Congress defined a new universal typology for new settlements, a minimum standard requirement for human space – on the housing scale as well as the urban one - and declared the abandonment of past models, considered to be expressions of bourgeois society, including the standard components of traditional urban design such as squares, parks, boulevards, and streets. The approach of CIAM III provided architects worldwide with a universal codex to develop the urban (and social) structure of the future; nevertheless, inspiration moved from a more technical point of view to a more political one. Even if the prime motivation for more healthy urban space for the working class, inspired by the recommendations in Friedrich Engels's book, was sincere, ideology sometimes drove further studies beyond the limit of scientific method. With the publication Großstadtarchitektur (1927), Ludwig Hilberseimer declared his open opposition to all traditional architecture that did not interpret the new Neue Sachlichkeit. Hilberseimer started from a criticism of the Siedlung to confirm the rigid application of the original principles of composition: high-rise blocks, standard linear housing units, repetition of floor plan to achieve the most effective performance in terms of costs and land consumption, serial and regular positioning of blocks, orientation along the solar path, suppression of any hierarchy in public space, breaking any direct relationship between building and street, repeatability and universality of typological schemes. Furthermore, the traditional opposition between city and countryside was easily overcome clearing away all elements that could have prevented a direct relationship with nature. The landscape became part of the city with no artificial opposition. Those principles of urban design rapidly became mainstream architectural thought worldwide, and manuals such as Ernst Neufert's Architect's Data (1936) confirmed this spreading trend. The book provided an ultimate source for the standardization of the entire human environment in all scales of design. It was an enormous success, translated into 18 languages and published in several editions; today it is still generally the most consulted building manual. Neufert added some diagrams for building orientation to help architects find the right solar orientation for blocks; nevertheless, until today no one has confirmed Heiligenthal-Gropius-Neufert's diagrams scientifically yet they were applied for years in many countries, dramatically influencing architects of the following generation.

In 1922, at the Salon d'Automne, seeking to refine his theory for the "machinist civilization", Le Corbusier presented his Ville Contemporaine de 3 millions d'habitants, and in 1925, his Plan Voisin for Paris; in 1930 Ville Radieuse was shown at the third CIAM in Brussels. The new modern urbanism standards set by L.C. between 1922 and 1930 were dramatically influenced by a desire to provide equal and better access to the sun in the apartment blocks; this was achieved by rotating the urban grid 19° northeast. This became "l'armature du tracé urbain."

Even in this case, L.C.'s proposal was not new from a technical point of view. In fact it derived directly from the heliothermic axis theory developed by Pidoux, Rey, and Barde published in 1928 in "La science des plans de Villes". According to Pidoux-Rey-Bardet's theory: "L'axe principal [of a building facade or city grid] au lieu d'être dirigé au sud est dévié vers l'ouest sous l'infuence de la température qui est plus élevéel'aprèsmidi que le matin et qui contribue à favoriser les valeurs héliothermiques de la deuxième moitié de la journée [...] Cette direction partage l'insolation totale en deux parties inégales et la valeur héhothermique totale en deux parties égales. Si nous supposons un bâtiment ou une suite de constructions alignées suivant cette direction, les façades tournées à l'est et celles tournées vers l'ouestjouiront de la même valeur héliothermique, savoir pour chacune la moitié de la valeur totale" ("The axis [of a building façade or urban grid] instead of being directed to south deflects westward under the influence of temperature. [The latter] is higher in the afternoon than in the morning and that raises solar thermal values during the second half of the day [...]. This orientation splits global exposure into two unequal parts and total heliothermic value into two equal parts. If we consider a building or a series of buildings aligned in this way, the façades facing east and west shall have the same heliothermic total that is the half of the total value each".

We should highlight the fact that Rey's studies concerned both the facade's sun lighting and temperature. The primary purpose of the heliothermic direction was to ensure the same thermal values on the west and east façades of a building during the day. According to geographic location, the direction can vary; for Paris, the city to which the study referred, the inclination is precisely 19° northeast. Rey drew both the "solar axis" and the "thermal axis," pointing out a discrepancy of 45° caused by the delay in the temperature trend, which reached its maximum values about three hours after midday (14:00–15:00). Thus, the heliothermic axis ensued from the bisecting line of the solar and thermal axes and, according to Rey, it would have taken advantage of the maximal annual solar radiation.

Twenty years later, the heliothermic theory began to be disputed. The opposing factions were the "hygienists," who were partisans of east-west exposure and the "climatologists," who tended to advocate a southern exposure. Among the latter were Bardet (1943), Vinaccia (1943), Hermant (1943), and Leroux (1946). Vinaccia's criticism mainly concerned the validity of the heliothermic unit, the results of thermal measurements on building surfaces and the lack of interest in other façades (southwest and northeast).

He declared the futility of this tool, considering it "one of the best-devised hoaxes," and accusing architects and planners of using it more for its novelty (and maybe for a political reason) than for its effectiveness.

A study conducted in 2005 by Harzallah et al. verified the heliothermic assumptions by comparing the temperatures and sun lighting values deduced from a building sample for the two orientations: north-south and 19° (Paris's heliothermic axis). The results showed that the heliothermic tilt causes a temperature increase of about 2 °C on the southeast façade, except in summer, and a decrease of 1–2 °C on the northwest one throughout the year. Conversely, heliothermic balance is achieved for the north-south orientation. Therefore, "L'égalité thermique moyenne, recherchée par les partisans de l'axe héliothermique, n'est donc réalisée que pour les façades exposées parfaitement à l'est et à l'ouest, c'est-à-dire pour un immeuble orienté exactement nord–sud. Toutes les autresorientations entraînent une dissymétrie thermique qui s'accroît au fur et à mesure que l'on s'écarte de l'axe Nord–Sud" ("The average thermal equality, sought by proponents of the heliothermic axis, is thus reached only for the façades that are oriented perfectly east and west, that is to say for a north-south oriented building. All other directions may cause thermal asymmetry that gradually increases as one moves away from the north-south axis").

In 2006, Steemers, Montavon, Cheng, and Compagnon carried out a similar study on the effectiveness of the heliothermic axis in La Ville Radieuse by Le Corbusier. They compared both the day-lighting potential of Le Corbusier's urban blocks (business and residential blocks) for two different orientations: north-south and heliothermic (19°, Paris) and the day-lighting potential of these with two different urban blocks in Paris at the time (~1920). In this case as well the project's assumptions about providing better access to the sun did not produce the sought-after results. Although daylight potential varied with the block typology and showed little increase in winter performance, generally the authors asserted "the effect of the heliothermic axis is negative as it results in smaller total illumination".

It is interesting to highlight that recent research has confirmed the inefficacy of Rey's theory and, while Vinaccia did not have the opportunity to apply contemporary research tools to his counter-theory, we are now able to confirm the correctness of his viewpoint.

Meanwhile, architecture and urban design were looking at new strategies to answer the need for hygiene in cities and another discipline began to adapt its perspective to the scale of the everyday human environment. In the very early period dating from the late nineteenth century to the late 1920s, the relationship between meteorology and architecture was discussed first by Schmauss in "Meteorologische Grundsätze im haus un Städtebau" (1914), and Kassner's "Die meteorologischen Grundlangen des Stadtebauliche Vortrage" (1910). Nevertheless, during this early phase, studies on cities and climate worldwide were mainly used to describe the modifications caused by each. In terms of the emergence of the new discipline of micro-climatology, the two decades between 1925 and the end of WWII, can be considered strategic. According to Fionn MacKillop, work on microclimatology and the urban climate increased significantly from 1960 onward but a significant peak of publication came about in the 1930s. The centre for these studies was Germany and Austria; in fact, German or Austrian scientists, a group of whom worked in Munich before 1934, produced a large number of papers. Despite never having been completed, the "Handbuch der Klimatologie in Fünf Bänden" (1927) by Rudolf Geiger (1894–1981), a meteorologist and climatologist, and the Russian Wladimir Peter Köppen (1846–1940), had broad resonance in the scientific debate at the time. Geiger's second book, "Das Klima der Bodennahen Luftschicht", translated in 1950 as Climate Near the Ground, is still considered a milestone in micrometeorology. The treatise describes how temperature, wind, and light can vary under the influence of ground form, vegetation, daylight, topography, and interrelations between humans and the microclimate. Nevertheless, in the early 1930s, the state of the art in the urban microclimate discipline was far from well established.

In the third period, up until World War II, urban climatic planning was seeking to become an autonomous discipline. Treatises gradually became more specific and systematic. Father Albert Kratzer's book Das Stadtklima (1937) is commonly considered the origin of the scientific debate on microclimate. Another German-born climatologist, Helmut Erich Landsberg, whose career developed in the U.S. after moving from Germany in 1934, does not mention the Geiger- Köppen works but refers directly to Kratzer's book even if most of the citations are climatic reports and statistical surveys, and some more related to fog, dust, or pollution prevention. However, despite the success of the topic among meteorologists, architects and planners, the book showed no signs of a comprehensive attempt to make connections between urban planning and microclimate. The contents of "The Climate of the Cities" provide only one direct suggestion for urban design, regarding the solar exposure of the city block; Kratzer mentioned Bernhard Christoph Faust's city plan dating from 1824. "The residential streets," said Kratzer, "run E–W, with all house-fronts facing south, so that each house may get as much sunlight as possible." In fact, aside from discussing building orientation, Faust (1755–1842) mostly referred to ancient Roman settlements. Even though he was a physician, he expressed his point of view through the Sonnenbaulehre theory. According to Plessner, who was Kratzer's source, Vitruvius largely inspired Faust. His Sonnenbau system (described in Faust's Andeutungen über das Bauen der Häuser und Städte zur Sonne) aimed at providing as much sun as possible to dwellings by planning settlements on a north-south grid and by ensuring a correct distance between the blocks. The Sonnenbau theory was supported by the Bayern architect, Gustav Vorherr (1778–1847). In 1818–1821, Vorherr designed the so-called "Sun Road," on the border between the ancient city centres of Munich and Ludwig. The road is strictly oriented to the south.

*

In 1925, the Italian Fascist party shifted from being just a social and political movement to a more organized structure coinciding with the central state, an institution requiring physical representation. Italian architects who were called upon to answer this request were divided between traditionalists and rationalists. Both factions aimed at capitalizing on the opportunity to provide an institutional style for the new regime. According to Manfredo Tafuri (1935–1994), the most inspired teams of the Italian Modern Movement was the so-called "Gruppo 7" founded 1926. Two years later the group expanded, and the MIAR (Movimento Italiano per l'Architettura razionale, Italian Movement for Rational Architecture) was founded, holding the first exhibition on rational architecture. Three years later, the so-called "Tavola degli orrori," was shown; it was a collage of the worst traditional architecture from the past. The two most important architectural journals, "Quadrante" (director, Bardi) and "Casabella" (director, Pagano), both supported the campaign against academic architecture, aiming to convince Mussolini to adopt the modern (international) style for public buildings. The traditionalists firmly opposed a movement that aimed at changing the status quo. In Milan, led by architects inspired by Camillo Sitte like Muzio, Greppi, and De Finetti, continued propounding their interpretation of the bourgeois city. In Rome, the conservative party in architecture led by Giovannoni, Foschini, Fasolo, and Del Debbio, supported by such magazines as La Ronda, Architettura e Arti decorative, and Valori Plastici, left no room for international-style theory. The bombastic praise of "being Italian" was taught in the architecture academies, and the scientific and pragmatic approach to building was methodically ignored to advance research on archaeology and antiquity as well as the promotion of national cultural heritage. Marcello Piacentini overcame the dualism between modern and traditional architecture. To give one example "Siamo d'accordo", he wrote: "ma i grandi monumenti romani e tutta l'architettura della Rinascenza [...] Non furono razionali, tutt'altro che razionali, decorative, formali, belli perché belli" ("We agree", he wrote, "but the great Roman monuments and all the architecture of the Renaissance [...] were not rational, far from rational, decorative, formal, beautiful just because they were beautiful"). Later, in his book "L'architettura di Oggi" (1930), he wrote "Il moderno in Italia si è fermato alle sole teorie semplificatrici. [...] Da noi l'ambientalismo e il carattere locale prendono il sopravvento sul tipo di edifcio. [...] Si confonde l'appellativo di –Italiano- con quello di "antico"; nella stessa maniera che si vuol far passare per straniero ogni tentativo di modernità" ("Modernism in Italy stopped with only some simplified theories. [...] Here contextualism and local character take over the building type [...] People confuse the epithet "Italian" with that of "antique"; in the same way, each attempt at modernism is considered as foreign").

Marcello Piacentini was able to manage this cultural duplicity for years; furthermore he interpreted the conservationist will of the Fascist party and consequently became the keystone of public policy on building. The so-called "School of Rome" monopolized the best opportunities and occupied the key positions in the cultural debate. Due to ignorance of modern architecture and its huge influence on contemporary architecture, Italian research in architecture was never linked to the most advanced international experiences. The publication of Giuseppe Samonà's book, La Casa Popolare degli anni '30 (1935) was an attempt to break out of this reactionary condition. Samonà, who later became Dean of the Venice School of Architecture, tried to focus on the topic of social housing which was driving his contemporaries in Europe to build the most inspiring architecture of the early twentieth century. Although Samonà's book can be easily considered the most advanced approach to the topic by Italian architects at the time, the book was largely ignored. Most probably, his explicit apology for socialist Karl Marx can explain such a general repulsion towards his work; nevertheless, despite the political context, this should not be the only reason to neglect it. In fact, the book contains and methodically organizes concepts that would have destabilized the mainstream and the organization of the entire Italian Architecture school system. Samonà's praise for Gropius, and his support for Klein's research on the minimum dwelling would have forced academics toward a more technical field and a more scientific approach. The E42 Exhibition Masterplan and the Milano Verde plan for the Sempione area in Milan (Albini,

Pagano, Gardella, Minoletti, Palanti Predeval, Romano, 1938) were the last two chances for Italian rationalist architecture to join the modern international movement. EUR 42 was completely directed and managed by Piacentini, who designed a monumental old-style scenario in which Rational architecture would have only been tasked with defining a bright image. Despite the fact that the "Milano Verde plan" has generally been considered the most important Italian contribution to European modern urban planning prior to World War II, the master plan did not have the same explicit content of the architecture to which it refers (Gropius and Hillberseimer), nor did it contain the same ideological character or radical perspective. The "Milano Verde plan" was seeking a balance between garden city models and linear high-rise buildings, between the Camillo Sitte's bourgeois city and the most advanced CIAM models. The result was a tempered proposal in which the radical repetition of standard typological configurations was not completely adopted; conversely, variety was desired and promoted. The application of Heiligenthal's rule and the orientation NE-SW of all the blocks on a grid oriented NW-SE (perpendicular to Corso Sempione) is the only explicit reference to the technical content of MM's research. With the exception of this citation, the project did not mention any study of the microclimate of urban space nor the healthiness of the proposal.

Der Untergang des Abendlandes (1918–1922) by Oswald Spengler, translated into Italian by the Fascist ideologue Julius Evola, described the West as though it were in a phase of its decay. The German philosopher also looked at the metropolis and materialism as the causes of this decline. This book had a strong influence on Mussolini's thought, so much so that the dictator initiated his anti-urban policies aimed at shaping Fascist society based on the family and craft guilds, reducing urban growth. Consequently, the theme of rationalization, standardization, and optimization of housing and urban transformation, characteristic of the 1920s in Europe, was narrowly expressed in Italy. Several new towns were founded to provide accommodations for the workforce for the mines (in Sardinia) and the countryside after land reclamation (in Lazio). Italian colonies in Africa also offered a new opportunity to explore spatial organization. In 1936, the VI Triennale di Milano, "Architettura rurale nel bacino del Mediterraneo" directed by Pagano moved the focus to vernacular architecture, seeking suggestions that would have led to a new Italian way towards rationalism.

It might be considered an attempt to interpret the spirit of the time, showing the architecture of the local past as genuine and practical.

Their perfect orientation and climate control offered the primary evidence for the rational approach of these buildings. "L'architettura rurale presenta evidenti legami con il suolo, con il clima, con l'economia e con la tecnica. Ne scaturiscono forme astratte e plastiche" ("Rural architecture has clear links with the land, climate, economy and with technology, [from that] abstract and plastic forms arise"). It can be read as the last attempt to provide a local version of the Neue Sachlichkeit without the application of the industrial process. In Costruzioni-Casabella, Irenio Diotallevi and Franco Marescotti, both Pagano's apprentices, published some evidence for the relationship between wellbeing and housing. These articles, collected in "Ordine e destino della casa popolare" (1941), sought to directly link illness and building form, focusing on the lack of insulation and ventilation as the main factors for the onset of disease in the working classes. Consequently, Diotallevi e Marescotti were considered the most important forerunners on the topic of building-related illness, reclaimed during the post WWII reconstruction phase. In 1948, the two architects published "Il problema sociale, costruttivo ed economico dell'abitazione" which mainly focused on the relationship of the topic to moral issues. Conversely in the "Il Manuale dell'Architetto," written in 1946 under Mario Ridolfi's supervision, it is easy to find a connection with the German experience, and issues of building orientation and ventilation were largely explained through graphics and diagrams. The scientific and pragmatic approach of Ridolfi's work appears similar to Neufert's Bauentwurfslehre (1936), which was published in Italy in 1946 as the "Enciclopedia pratica del progettare e costruire." Architecture played no direct social role in this manual; it was considered to be merely a problem of technical knowledge. Even if the authors knew the work of Klein, Gropius, and Hillberseimer well, they aimed to move the Italian debate on housing to more advanced issues relating to human health.

*

According to Cesare Silvi, who had direct access to Vinaccia's archive, Gaetano Vinaccia was born in Naples in 1889. Due to family problems, he obtained his education in the field. In 1909, Vinaccia was awarded a high school diploma at the Brescia Technical Institute. In 1917, he achieved the qualification as Professor of Architectural Drawing and between 1919 and 1926, he published some minor books on historic heritage, antiquity, and archaeology. In 1926 he graduated in civil engineering from the University of Freiburg; then in 1930 he was appointed to teach technical drawing at a local high school in Rome. During his stay in Rome, his interest in insulation increased dramatically; between 1935 and 1943, he published several works in which he attempted to play a role in the international debate.

We can recognize four different phases in Vinaccia's work. From 1919 until 1926–27, he applied his knowledge to the field of architecture, achieving only mediocre success. He had some minor work opportunities in Rome (on Via Monteverdi, Rome, 1918) that would hardly have given him a chance to be recognized in the complicated milieu of Italian architecture in the 1920s and 1930s. The period from 1926 to 1930, corresponding to his stay in Freiburg, can be considered the most fruitful period of his life. In fact, he had the opportunity to join most advanced research in architecture, meteorology and civil engineering. During his stay in Rome he was member of the board of a minor architectural magazine: "Case d'oggi" and during this third period he tried to influence the debate on typology led by rationalist architects worldwide. During the last phase, which can be considered the mature point of his career, Vinaccia tried to move toward an Italian approach to urban microclimate design with the publication of his most cited work, "La Città di Domani, Come il clima plasma la forma urbana e l'architettura: la sanità e l'igiene cittadina" ,Vol. 1 (1943).

During his stay in Freiburg, Gaetano Vinaccia was dramatically influenced by the German cultural context. The Bavarian milieu offered many suggestions, both regarding the urban microclimate as well as modern architecture, with such personalities as Schmauss, Köppen, Geiger, Kratzer (the meteorologist), and Theodor Fisher, who, as previously mentioned, was a professor at the Technical University of Munich and leader of Deutscher Werkbund. Therefore both Fisher's Alte Heide Plan and Otto Heasler's Georgsgarten Siedlung should have been well known to Vinaccia as a student. Moreover, his knowledge of the German language could have given him direct access to Heiligenthal's Deutsche Städtebau (1921).

At the time of his return to Italy, three CIAMs had been held. As stated, the second addressed typology, and the third urbanism. Not surprisingly, Vinaccia's published work followed that same order; and even if it still reveals an exciting modernity, Vinaccia's cultural relevance was neglected both as an architect and as an *ante litteram* microclimate urban designer. In 1936, Vinaccia had not yet written the best of his scientific work and he clearly knew that, within the Italian framework, he had only one option: to convince the establishment that his scientific theories did not contrast with the mainstream, but could conversely support the Fascist rhetoric of the supposed superiority of Roman civilization. Thus his pioneering spirit was always mixed with a proud sense of belonging to local architectural traditions, placing him in an intermediate position that could not have had any appeal for the European Modern Movement's inner circle, or even for the more up-to-date Italian publications. On the other hand, his scientific point of view would have appeared obscure to most Italian architects, whose academic approach to architectural issues by no means included technical content. Therefore, it was between the 1930s and 1940s, when Piacentini's leadership emerged radically on the Italian scene, that Vinaccia started to find a place for his proposals, mixing his knowledge of antiquity and his ability in the field of engineering to support an Italian path toward modern architecture.

After World War II anyone who was considered to be making compromises with the past began to be ignored. The Roman cultural circle, which revolved around Piacentini's controversial personality, was blamed for Italy's alleged backwardness in relation to international Modern Movement innovations. Moreover, general interest in microclimatic effects on buildings dramatically declined until the 1970s so that the first modern organic treatises on urban microclimatology are still considered to be Oke's work and Landsberg's "The Urban Climate", 1981 (MacKillop), even if neither were architects and had no chance of directly influencing architecture and urbanism. Therefore, when Vinaccia coined the definition "Polis-climatologia" (from the Greek πόλις pólis]-κλίνω [clìno]-λόγος [logos]) in his "La Città di Domani, Vol. 1" (1943), he was an absolute innovator.

The question of whether Vinaccia can be considered an innovator or not is largely based on the point of view of architectural criticism. In order to look at Vinaccia's role in history from the correct perspective, we may consider that, until World War II, his contribution did not lie within a well-defined discipline in which it could be classified. Nonetheless, he was fully aware of his professional fate when, in 1936 he wrote: "É utile nei riguardi dell'urbanistica fare alcuni raffronti concreti, fra i vari tipi di case, quelle di oggidì e quelle che auspichiamo per un domani molto prossimo, quando la forza delle cose trionferà ineluttabilmente sul misoneismo e al solito i misoneisti si daranno aria di precursori speculando sul frutto dei pionieri che diventeranno per essi dei passatisti" ("On urbanism we should take into account some comparisons between different housing typologies, all those of today and all those we wish for in the immediate future, when the strength of things will inevitably win over misoneism and [when], as usual, the misoneists will strut around their forerunners, taking advantage of the fruits of those pioneers who will be considered as lovers of the past".).

Vinaccia's desire to influence the cultural debate in Italy moved him to publish several articles during his stay in Rome. With the title "Progetto di casa economica", he published his scheme for the pentagonal and heptagonal star-shaped house in "L'Architettura Italiana" (1932) and "Case d'Oggi" (1936). The earlier purpose was to rationalize interior space in order to gain economic, aesthetic, and hygienic advantages. The "star-shaped" (pentagonal or heptagonal) building offered the possibility to serve 10 or 14 apartments per floor with a single staircase. Furthermore, the star-shaped plan guaranteed three different exposures for each flat, taking advantage of interior natural ventilation and sunlight. The use of a glass skylight on the roof would also have contributed to entry and stairwell ventilation and lighting. The effectiveness of the skylight had already been confirmed in Vinaccia's previous successful work in Rome (1918: house in Via C. Monteverdi, no. 20).

Seven months after its publication, the author compared the urban layout of star-shaped buildings with others composed of different building typologies. The comparison also took into account planning fees and construction costs. Here Vinaccia clearly referred to Le Corbusier's cross-shaped skyscrapers but his proposal sought to develop the concept on a technical level. Nonetheless, the author supported the Modern Movement theory of urbanism in proclaiming his preference for high-rise buildings. According to the author: "Scopo del presente studio è quello di richiamare l'attenzione degli edili sulla necessità della esatta conoscenza del moto apparente del sole per razionalizzare in unione alla attinometria ed alla tecnica dell'illuminazione e dell'isolamento termico, l'urbanistica [...] dando seria base scientifca ai regolamenti edilizi, spesso arbitrari ed irrazionali" ("The purpose of this study is to call architects' attention to the knowledge of the sun's illusory motion in order to rationalize urban planning [...], giving a serious scientific basis to building codes, which are often arbitrary and irrational").

In 1937, Gaetano Vinaccia published "Il corso del sole in urbanistica ed in edilizia. Contributo alla razionalizzazione dell'architettura", Hoepli. As declared in the title, his attempt was to steer the debate on architecture and planning to a more rational and technical field. The book is divided into six sections. The first three, characterized by more technical content, offer graphics that provide basic information on sun paths (trajectory, height, and azimuth), sunlight of building surfaces, and related thermal effects.

The fourth and fifth chapters deal with sunlight in planning and architecture, defining both the best orientation and proportions in the "Urban Program for Sunlighting". The latter is defined by local climate and latitude.

Vinaccia also examined the effects of sunlight/shading on building surfaces determined by urban street grids having different orientations and ratios (H/W ratio) at different latitudes. An in-depth examination of 30 Italian cities with an "equisolare plan" closes the urban section. Concerning the studies on the urban block, the author investigated the orientation and interior arrangement of buildings in relation to sun paths and building use. The last section deals with the use of solar heating in agriculture (solar greenhouses) and in domestic central heating systems. The study was innovative for its time, providing interesting thoughts on energy and economic gains relating to the passive exploitation of the sun in those countries located in advantageous climates such as Italy and the Italian African colonies of the past. What emerges from the text is the author's up-to-date technical and interdisciplinary knowledge. The bibliography mainly presents texts on meteorology, physics, and astronomy, but Vinaccia's attention to global studies emerges notably, especially regarding the French research on the heliothermic axis by A. Rey and Brooks's studies (Berkeley, California)

Two years later in the manuscript "Rationality of the Romans' Castra" (1939), Vinaccia analysed the orientation of ancient Roman settlements with the purpose of showing that Roman settlements were the most rational urban design for contemporary city planning.

The author claimed that religious dogmas and rituals did not determine a city's position and orientation. In fact he stated that the N–S and E–W directions of the city axes originated in rational motives more related to the need for protection from bothersome, unhealthy winds, and to the need for optimal sunlight use. In reference to the writings of classical authors (Vitruvius, De Architettura; Vegezio, Institutorium rei militaris ex commentariis Catonis, Celsi, Trajani, Hadriani et Frontini; Varrone, De Re Rustica; Columella, De Re Rustica; Hygini Gromantici, De Castris Romanis) Vinaccia highlighted their surprising approach to managing the effects both of the wind and the sun on cities' degrees of comfort on different latitudes. With regard to the urban-scale analysis, the author noted that Roman Italian cities show a deviation of about 30° from the N–S axis to protect from both cold N–NW winds and the unhealthy and wet S–SE winds. Moreover, this orientation guarantees sufficient sunlight on all four building surfaces.

The book "La Città di Domani" (1943) sought to promote awareness of city planning in order to instruct technicians on design and health-related building issues. The new discipline born from the fusion of planning and microclimatology, which Vinaccia called "polisclimatology", would have supported architects both in making the correct location choice for a city's foundation and in modelling urban form. The author analysed the main meteorological phenomena andhighlighted their physical causes, benefits and harm to human health, relationships with the built environment and solutions used throughout history (contained both in vernacular examples and in ancient documents by Vitruvius, Hippocrates, etc.).

On the topic of solar radiation, which the author developed in previous publications, Vinaccia analysed the effect of atmospheric moisture, fog, rain, pressure, winds, electric fields, and the ionization of air on people and the urban environment. Regarding wind, Vinaccia proposed the foundation of "Urban Anemometry", an approach that would have been able to provide reliable data regarding the speed and frequency of winds in urban areas. Concerning the sun, Vinaccia resumed his "Urban Program for Sunlighting" in relation to the three recognized climates (equatorial, intertropical, and temperate); he expounded his theory on "equisolar orientation" for the "equalization of sunlight among all the four sides of a cubic block", clearly in opposition to the heliothermic axis theory by Rey, Barde, and Pidoux (1928), also abandoned by Le Corbusier in the 1940s. The text ends with a chapter on the microclimatic benefits of green areas in urban space and an annex on more specific topics such as the quality of soil, drinking water, sewerage, and building codes.

The content of his work make the author extremely modern and even if he played a minor role at the time, there are several reasons to reconsider his scientific contribution. Among these is Vinaccia's forward look to the founding of "polisclimatology" as a link between planning and microclimatology. Unfortunately, as previously stated, the cultural and historic context was not favourable to its dissemination. Moreover, after the World War II, the "bioclimatic" approach was overwhelmed by the large-scale use of technology in building, a trend that went on until the 1960s. It was only in the 1970s–1980s, with the international oil crisis and looming environmental disaster (global warming, 1986; hole in the ozone layer, 1985, etc.) that "bioclimatism" caught on. It seems interesting that in 1981, Lansberg still declared a lack of dialogue between planners and meteorologists, which began, according to Givoni, only in 1998. In this light, Vinaccia appears to have been a pioneer. In fact, while most of Vinaccia's theories were already known in distinct international scientific circles, he was perhaps the first to organize them into a systematic approach, thanks also to his education as an architect, which contributed to a more humanistic idea of architecture and planning. From this perspective, urban microclimatology represents an additional field to take into consideration in urban design.

Basically, the technical notions contained in Vinaccia's writings (which concerned physics, astronomy, and meteorology) were well known since ancient times and were included in fundamental texts such as Hippocrates' On Air, Water and Places and Vitruvius' *De Architettura*. Nevertheless, his contribution appears to have been innovative because he seems to reveal several important issues relating to microclimatic urban design despite the fact that he could

not achieve the same in-depth scientific analysis as current research. Today, after 50 years of scientific progress these can be considered milestones in the development of today's "environmental design.
Among these we should mention the following topics:
• The role of sky turbidity (air pollution and haziness) in reducing the duration of sunshine in urban areas. Vitruvius addressed the importance of sky clarity for urban health. But only after the Industrial Revolution with the desperate conditions of urban pollution did scientists study the effects of pollutants on solar radiation, revealing its weakened intensity and its decreased daily duration. Quantitative studies on the topic were already contained in Kratzer's "Das Stadtklima" (1937), and Chandler (1965) and Landsberg (1981) later conducted exhaustive studies. Contemporary research includes "the extinction coefficient" by Givoni and the urban studies carried out by both Tsangrassoulis on solar short-wave radiation and by Santamouris on the city's thermal balance, which are contained in Energy and Climate in the Urban Built Environment.
• The effect of latitude on the total amount of solar radiation received on building surfaces due to different sun paths. As stated, for a long time Vinaccia's studies focused on sun paths and solar radiation. These produced useful measurements and tools, mainly collected in his text "Il corso del sole in Urbanistica e in Edilizia" (1938). Today, the study of local sun paths and the tilt angle of the sun are among the first procedures undertaken in environmental design. Nevertheless, architects and planners have at their disposal sun charts, which graphically depict both the sun's height and azimuth, as well as a collection of meteorological data regarding the intensity of solar radiation in function of location.
• The effect of topography and orientation of building surfaces on microclimate. Vinaccia was already aware of the environmental factors that cause fog and increase moisture in urban areas, such as proximity to water (sea, lake, river, etc.) and the thermo-hygrometric conditions of the ground. He also knew the effects of topography both on the formation of the "cold side rain" and "hot side rain" on slopes, and the wind's speed and alterations of direction (the Venturi effect). He identified the south-facing slope of a hill as a suitable location for ensuring building health; this position takes advantage of direct solar gain and better natural ventilation, avoiding the shadows of buildings and the stagnation of fog and moisture. Several contemporary authors who suggest this location, especially in temperate climates, confirm the microclimatic advantage of the south-facing slope of a mountain. It can be found in most later research: Oke's "Boundary

Layer Climate" (1978) and Givoni's "Climate Consideration in Building and Urban Design" (1998), are both reference books for most current scholars, but they restate most of Vinaccia's points almost 40 years later with a more in-depth scientific analysis.

According to Vinaccia, architects and planners have three main tools for pursuing a city's health (also intended to secure people's physical and psychological well-being):
1. Appropriate settlement location;
2. Accurate choice of building morphology;
3. Correct use of both building materials and exterior textures.

On the first point, Vinaccia refused any standard approach to architecture design and planning. Conversely, in his opinion, the suitable location of a city is based on local microclimatic factors and topography, which contribute to defining appropriate local environmentally friendly architecture and urban form. This led Vinaccia to define his "Urban Program for Sunlighting" according to local climatic specificity. Vinaccia's program was also developed in relation to his research on vernacular architecture in different climates, such as the Arab city in a hot climate, the courtyard house in temperate zones, and the villa in a cold climate.

Certainly after the VI Triennale di Milano led by Pagano in 1936, the national focus moved toward vernacular architectural solutions. Moreover colonial expansion in the twentieth century contributed greatly to Vinaccia's interest in the equatorial-tropical climate and vernacular typologies. These studies suggested low-tech and low-energy-cost architectural solutions as far back as the 1940s. After the oil crisis in the 1970s, several studies also approached vernacular architecture aiming at re-evaluating past lessons and bio-architectural practices in order to contribute to global energy-savings and environmental goals. A far-ranging bibliography exists on this topic. Contemporary examples can be found in the writings of Steemers and Azami on the "environmental" lessons of the past traditions. On a similar topic, research by Oliver, Vellinga, and Fernandes and Matheus on the "sustainable" practices of vernacular architecture, and the work of Caltabiano on Matmata dwellings and Sicilian traditional architecture are worth considering. Finally, climatic features couple with energy perspectives in the work of Coch Roura Gallo and Los on traditional habitat and architecture.

In all of his publications, Gaetano Vinaccia highlighted the importance of building morphology and its relationship to the environmental context. In particular he studied the role of the so called "urban canyon", taking into consideration the relationship between building height and street width (aspect ratio), and street and building geometry in relation to solar radiation penetration (sky view factor) which are both still considered to be two of the most common ratios in environmental parameters. The author used those two factors to examine urban ventilation and sun lighting in relation to latitude and altitude, in order to identify the most suitable and effective building orientation to ensure appropriate layout of interior and exterior building spaces. According to Vinaccia, the best orientation for sun lighting means guaranteeing, "on equal sun lighting, the shortest distance among buildings and the greater height of these, thus greater building density". As mentioned, land use efficiency was a fundamental issue during the Modern Movement and it has continued to be central after the 1960s in contemporary research. Martin and March conducted an important study at the University of Cambridge on land-use optimality, which has recently been extended to broader environmental questions by Steemers, Ratti, and Raydan.

Furthermore, images and theories contained in "La Città di Domani Vol.1", suggest that Vinaccia was aware of several technical issues, like the "vertical air-film" developed in proximity of building surfaces. In his drawings, he referred to the "street's cross-ventilation due to sun lighting", highlighting the circular motion caused by surface temperatures and street orientation. The scientific progress of the last 60 years has allowed this to be verified through quantitative analyses and measurements.

The latest studies by Santamouris and Erell regarding air-film on a building's façade are significant. Finally, it is important to highlight the fact that Vinaccia was a pioneer in the use of technical tools to support urban design, and in the study of the sun's path and direct solar radiation. He suggested two useful systems to consider a site's annual sun lighting: overview photographs, shot every half-hour during solstices and equinoxes, and the poliseliometro, "a device specifically created to test building models through artificial sun lighting". This tool was useful to the author in understanding the sun's profile on building surfaces. Today, this task is entrusted to software, and there is abundant reference literature on the topic, among which Robinson, Beckers, Badea, and Lim et al.

The interdisciplinary knowledge of the author allowed him to connect physical theories to architectural practice. He knew the "Beer–Lambert Law" and the "Cosine Law" (both still included in Oke's writings 35 years later), recommending both surface inclination and its geometry as additional design strategies to limit the intensity of direct solar radiation and, thus, decrease surface temperature. On the basis of these studies, a curved surface improves radiation dispersion, decreasing the thermal effects of sunlight. Compared with a flat surface, the reduction ranges from 0.50 in the case of a sphere to 0.58 for a horizontal cylinder.

One of the goals of modern architecture was to ensure an appropriate amount of sun, air, and light in buildings. After the 1960s, the question changed to the issue of what form architecture and the city should have to become "efficient", or rather to pursue energy-saving goals and pollution containment. During the 1980s, research and design contests relating to the passive exploitation of the sun increased swiftly. In 1984, Gupta studied the solar efficiency of archetypal building clusters taking into account the solar exposure of building surfaces. Some years later, in 1987, the same clusters were evaluated for their thermal efficiency and comfort. Gupta's studies also referred to Knowles's work on the "solar envelope". The American researcher published "Sun Rhythm Form" in 1985 to study the link between "building groups and the resultant solar shading from the point of view of maximizing winter solar heat gain while minimizing it in summer". Knowles's reasons for studying solar access, which concern the support of and increase in quality of life (also in the sense of wellbeing) appear to meet Vinaccia's thought on some points. In 1986, S. Owens analysed the link between energy sources and the city's spatial structure recognizing urban context, orientation, layout, and density as significant variables in a building's energy behaviour. In Hawkes' "The Environmental Tradition" (1996), alternative building forms for exploiting solar heat were also analysed. During the last 20 years, scientific progress both in computer science and CFD systems has produced useful technological tools with which researchers can evaluate and compare the environmental behaviour of different buildings and urban forms, including airflows and human thermal comfort. Literature and international research programs on this topic are abundant.

In order to improve (or reduce) surface thermal effects caused by solar radiation, Vinaccia suggested the correct use of building materials as a way of taking advantage of its properties. The author was well aware both of the albedo as a theoretical and practical construct, and the characteristics of materials that affect radiation thermal absorption or emission, such as surface colours and texture. Vinaccia's reported studies had already stated the contribution of the façade's roughness to the reduction of surface temperature due to increased shading. In Vinaccia's writings, attention to surface materials and the corresponding albedo values extended to the building context. Vinaccia used the example of Cefalù (Sicily) to illustrate the influence of the surrounding environment on urban microclimatic behaviour. The small Sicilian city is situated against a high grey rock face that reflects sunlight and heat onto buildings year-round. In Vinaccia's opinion, in order to enhance urban comfort, it was necessary to change the face's albedo, covering the rock with green and exploiting local sea breezes during the afternoon. Similar research and recommendations are widespread today, and entire book sections are dedicated to the characteristics of materials and comparison of albedo values. Both Santamouris and Givoni devote important sections to the thermal properties of building materials. Several other studies can be added to these; the albedo value has become a central parameter in the study of urban energy balance and heat mitigation strategies (Santamouris; Taleghani et al.; Giridharan and Kolokotroni).

Two last brief points suggest considering Vinaccia as a pioneer in this field.

The first concerns the influence of green areas on the urban microclimate. He examined the cooling action of vegetation due to metabolism as well as the low albedo values of greenery. This theory has been extensively proved starting in the 1970s. Reference studies from the 1980s are contained in Oke's Boundary Layer Climates ("Clothesline-effect", "Leading-edge or fetch effect", and "Oasis-effect" of vegetation) and Landsberg's "The Urban Climate". Moreover, contemporary research includes the work of Erell, Santamouris, and Costa and Loures.

A second point is his warning regarding the lack of climatic data in urban areas. Vinaccia noted that data is indispensable for urban design and planning. In particular, he encouraged the collection of airflow data in urban space. This is an issue still debated today, with a slow increase in data collection through surveys (local measurement campaigns) and database implementation such as GIS (Niachou et al.); Tsouchlaraki et al.).

In light of the facts, even if the validity of Vinaccia's intuitions and their actual correspondence with the most current research are still to be investigated in subsequent studies, today we can state that the content of his better-known theoretical works seemed to reflect full awareness of the main issues relating to the topic as early as the 1940s. Therefore, the most brilliant contribution of Vinaccia's work was his determination to found a new discipline, which he called "polisclimatology" and which would have changed the general approach to urbanism, and his attempt to relate architecture and town planning to urban physics. Despite the fact that the theories cited by Vinaccia were already known in the scientific community and some were well known since ancient times, he was able to collect them in a complete study. He gave architects a chance to link their work to microclimate, comfort, and illness, topics reinforcing a humanistic idea of architecture and planning. From this perspective, urban microclimatology does not represent merely an additional scientific field to take into account but a different theoretical approach to human environmental design.

Today, when environmental and bioclimatic questions are posed with great force in architecture and planning, the re-evaluation of Vinaccia's work might be useful by influencing the architectural debate on sustainable development and urban growth and by filling that gap in the dialogue between planners and meteorologists which Lansberg decried in 1981.

DEUTSCHER STÄDTEBAU

EIN HANDBUCH FÜR ARCHI-
TEKTEN · INGENIEURE ·
VERWALTUNGSBEAMTE
U. VOLKSWIRTSCHAFTLER
VON ROM. HEILIGENTHAL
DR. ING. DR. RER. POL. MAGISTRATSBAURAT

HEIDELBERG 1921 · BEI CARL WINTER

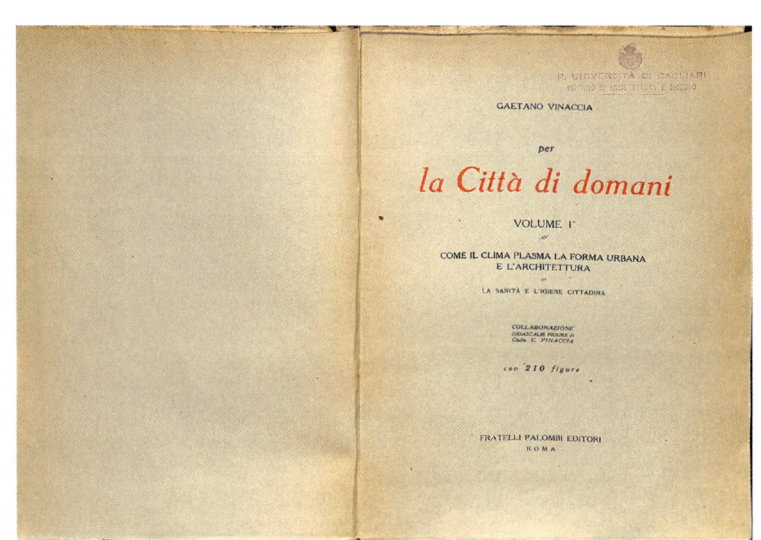

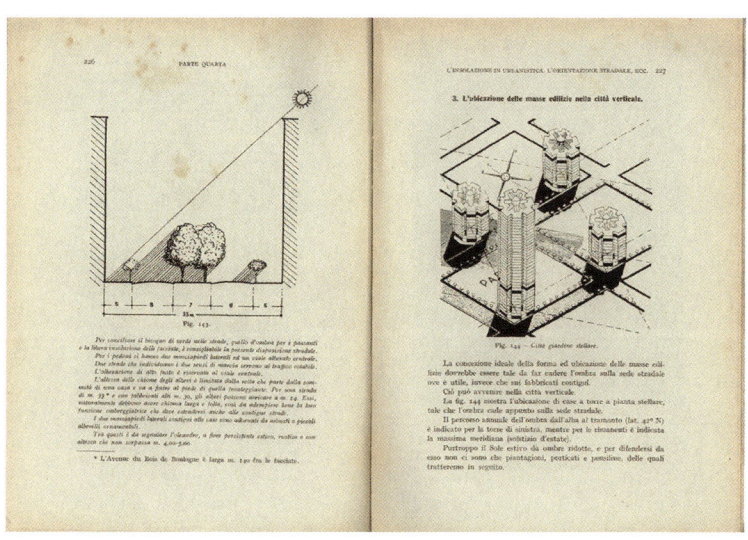

Fig. 143.

Fig. 144. — Città giardino stellare.

3. L'ubicazione delle masse edilizie nella città verticale.

Per conciliare il bisogno di varchi nelle strade, pozzi d'ombra per i fusserelli e la libera insolazione delle facciate, è consigliabile la potente disposizione stradale. Due i pedoni ci hanno due marciapiedi laterali ed un viale alberato centrale. Due strade che individuano i due sensi di marcia avranno al traffico centrale. L'ubicazione di alti fusti è riservata al viale centrale. L'altezza delle cimose degli alberi è limitata dalla sorte che i parte della comunità di uno caso e un a fianco al piede di quelli prospicienti. Per una strada di m. 35* e con fabbricati alti m. 30, gli alberi possono arrivare a m. 24. Essi, visivamente difendono meno chiesa largo e tolto, così dei intomino loro le loro funzione ombreggiante che deve estendersi anche alle contigue strade. I due marciapiedi laterali contigui alla case sono utilizzati da salotti e piccoli alberelli ornamentali.

Tra questi i due argomenti d'intervento, si fanno persistente estivo, rustico a non odore che non sorpassa m. 4,00-5,00.

L'Avenue du Bois de Boulogne è larga m. 140 fra le facciate.

La concezione ideale della forma ed ubicazione delle masse edilizie dovrebbe essere tale da far cadere l'ombra sulla sede stradale ove è utile, invece che sui fabbricati contigui.

Ciò può avvenire nella città verticale.

La fig. 144 mostra l'ubicazione di case a torre a pianta stellare; tale che l'ombra cade appunto sulla sede stradale.

Il percorso annuale dell'ombra dall'alba al tramonto (lat. 42° N) è indicato per le torre di sinistra, mentre per le circostanti è indicata la massima meridiana (solstizio d'estate).

Purtroppo il Sole estivo dà ombre ridotte, e per difendersi da esso non ci sono che piantagioni, porticati e parasolare, delle quali tratteremo in seguito.

"It is not history and age, but structure, ideas and ecology that give quality to an urban context"

Leon Krier

CHAPTER **FIVE**

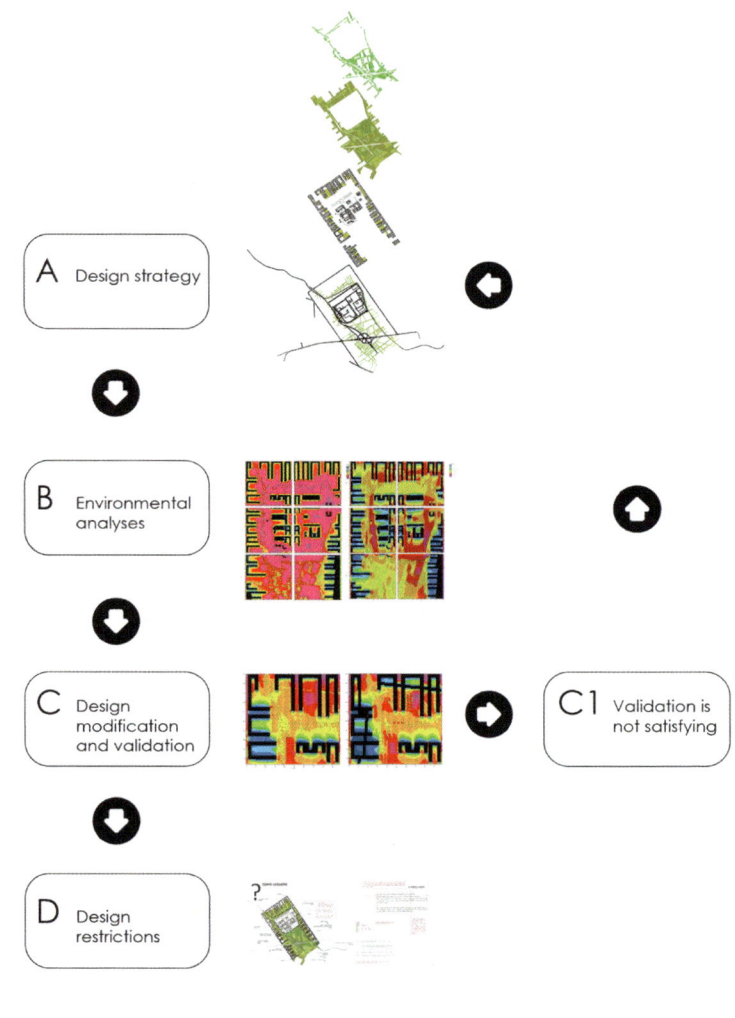

Workflow

Chapter FIVE

Practices

In the previous chapters, we illustrated the direct relationship between urban form and local microclimate. This mutual influence has largely been ascertained; it can significantly affect building performance in terms of comfort and energy consumption (Carmeliet et al., 2013; Blocken, 2012; Steemers et al., 2006; Ratti et al., 2006; Givoni, 1998). These studies have also highlighted the importance of broadening design to include the urban dimension (De Pascali, 2008; Fraker, 2013). During the 1970s, the EU commission stated that urban design was the appropriate tool for achieving sustainability goals. Current 'sustainable urban design' is characterized by the complex contribution of different disciplines. This interdisciplinary perspective and the need for incorporating external contributions has led to updated design approaches while maintaining architecture at the core of the process. The Monserrato master plan tests a methodology that integrates environmental data and analyses, starting with the initial design phases. Such software as Heliodon and ENVImet, which acted as useful 'feedback' tools to verify –qualitatively - the environmental impact of the design concept, supported the design process. In particular, the environmental analyses focused on the microclimatic consequences of urban form, taking into account different climatic data and formal parameters. The initial urban proposal was gradually modified and re-evaluated several times in relation to the main criticalities emerging from the results of the analyses compared with comfort standards contained in bio-climatic diagrams (Olgyay). Nevertheless, the modifications were in line with the fundamental concepts of the master plan and contributed to improving overall performance.

The case study concerned a new urban design for the area near the university district of Monserrato, called the 'Cittadella'. The proposal sought to combine the demands expressed by the citizenry, contained in the documents for the management and organization of the township (P.U.C., Strategic Plan; V.A.S., etc.) with the energy and environmental needs of 'eco-sustainable' urban development.

The main issues faced in the project were:

• The physical and functional reconnection between the City and the Cittadella, which is clearly separated by the 554 Road.
• The expansion of services and functions strongly related to the university.
• The containment of urban and suburban sprawl.
• Respect for the agricultural vocation of the land.

With these preliminary observations, the project created a new urban district occupying an area of about 1.4 km2. The new district placed buildings along the outer edge of the area surrounding the Cittadella, which is located in the centre of the system. It reconnects with the north-western outskirts of the city of Monserrato along the south side. A large urban park characterized by different densities and gradients of green space connects the two systems, Cittadella and the new area of growth, to one another. The outer edge of the design creates an anti-sprawl system detectable in its unity on the territorial scale. It aims to contain future urban growth in the surrounding areas. This border clearly characterizes the relationship between interior and exterior space of the built context which is strengthened by using the "C" block whose central courtyard is oriented towards the park and the Cittadella. The maximum height of the blocks remains constant throughout the master plan: on one side, this choice underlines once again the territorial scale and on the other it rooted the project to the ground allowing us to read its slope. The continuous ground elevation to the north, in fact, reduces the overall height of the blocks, which slowly penetrate the ground, thus dialoguing coherently with the upper front, still used for agriculture.

The park grid based on the lots of the pre-existing agricultural fields evidences the importance of agriculture, which is still present in the area. The traces/marks of the pre-existing fields now accommodate walking and cycling paths and enclose new green areas, such as alternating lawns, gardens and trees, with different densities in relation to the proximity to the main thoroughfares and to different functions.

The connections between the different levels, the central park and the outer streets, on which the blocks are placed, are resolved through the bases of the blocks themselves. The opening of the inner courtyards toward the central park folds/bends the base toward the green areas, thus defining two different public spaces within the same court: a central square, located in the nearest part to the building, and an inclined plane, characterized by an intermediate gradient of green, that connects the square and the park.

The blocks have different sizes ranging from 50 to about 200m; the inner spaces and their mutual distances are designed in order to ensure a mix of functions within 400m and the possibility to reach the light rail line and university buildings by foot. In addition, the potential to capture and exploit renewable sources offered by the central park and the roofs of the buildings, together with their location around a central core, makes the new area similar to an "autonomous district" within a broader territorial network.

The process adopted in this case is similar to the procedures used in recent years in some European research. However, it differs because this work does not apply the process to an existing fabric, but rather to a new urban design, using different software. The methodology can be summarized as follows:

1. Design of a preliminary proposal;
2. Microclimatic analysis of spatial configurations, taking into consideration the climatic conditions of the site in order to identify the main critical situations;
3. Modification of the initial design proposal according to improvements on the former criticalities;
4. Microclimatic verification of the new improved contributions;
5. Definition of the final satisfactory design solution.

As previously mentioned, the study of the microclimatic interactions between urban form and local weather/environmental site conditions took into consideration seven main parameters:

• Morphological: the aspect ratio (H/W), orientation and the sky view factor (SVF);

• Environmental: temperature (°C), relative humidity (%), wind speed (m/s) and direction (deg°), direct solar radiation (kWh/m^2).

Analysis assessed the performance of environmental parameters in relation to the more critical days of the year (the solstices) and was developed through the use of two specific software programs: ENVI-met and Heliodon. In particular, the first took into consideration: relative humidity, temperature, wind speed and direction, and SVF; while the second took into account: direct solar radiation and shading. Climatic data was collected from three main sources: E.E.R.E. of the U.S Department of Energy (IWEC data); Meteotest (Meteonorm v.6.1 database) and A.R.P.A.S. Specialist Department of Sardinia Region.

The results of the environmental analysis point out the main criticality in the upper part of the master plan (sectors C1 and C2), especially during the summer. In fact, the study of maps in relation to the local Mediterranean climate reveals two main critical points:

• The high wind speed in the courtyards of the N-W buildings. Although the data does not highlight dangerous situations, the ability of the wind to reach its maximum intensity warns against possible discomfort in these areas. Surveys conducted by the regional environmental department (ARPAS) on the prevailing winds in the area showed the predominance of cold, high intensity winds (> 13m/s) during the winter and medium-intensity (8-13 m/s) during the summer.

The real wind values, much higher than the input data used for the calculation, show these areas to have a potential situation of great discomfort, also confirmed by recent studies and research on wind patterns in urban areas. In fact, according to the statements by V. Olgyay, a person feels a 'windy' condition when wind speed is from 2-3 m/s; if this value reaches 5 m/s, only 6% of people define the situation acceptable while the 65% will definitely define it uncomfortable, or even dangerous.

• The great amount of direct solar radiation on public space surfaces. Also in this case, the broader debate on local climatic conditions helps us understand the importance of this parameter on outdoor comfort. According to the Köppen classification, a "hot summer" is characteristic of this place. The great amount of radiation recorded by the software during the summer, combined with a large number of hours, shows how the surfaces of the inner courts may, in reality, appear particularly uncomfortable during the summer. In fact, their large size and the absence of a shading system expose their surfaces to direct radiation throughout the entire day. Moreover, the greater height and proximity of the sun rays reduces the shadows cast on the ground, leaving most of the surface exposed to sunlight, thus increasing the radiation absorbed by the ground and thus overall temperatures.

The Olgyay bioclimatic chart was used to assess the degree of comfort provided by the project during the summer; along with the daily average values detected by the software, it reported the monthly average data. Furthermore, the master plan was divided into three main sectors according to the prevalent orientation of blocks: S-W, N-W, N-E, in order to better understand the consequence of morphology on microclimatic effects.

• The N-W blocks reach extremely high temperatures fostered by their orientation, which allows the sun penetration during the entire day. According to chart, the court needs a wind speed of over 3m/s to provide a minimum degree of comfort. Despite the seasonal presence of medium-strong winds, such speed does not guarantee comfort conditions for people.

• The different orientation of the S-W blocks means that it has an average daily temperature slightly lower than the former because of the shadows cast by buildings on the central area. However, the data on temperature and humidity detected by the project, does not guarantee human comfort, requiring in this case minimum ventilation a bit higher than 3 m/s. The intensity recorded in the courtyards currently remains below this value: 0.9-2m/s; however, the constant presence during the year of strong-medium intensity wind suggests acceptable average weather conditions for the use of outdoor space.

• The N-E blocks are the only blocks that can ensure, in their current state, a sufficient degree of environmental comfort. The highest aspect ratio values determine greater shading of central surfaces providing increased relief during the summer season. Their proximity to the main air-path of the master plan also guarantees the necessary ventilation for human comfort in the courts.

In light of the above considerations, the 'corrective' actions taken on the initial project were mainly focused on the N-W blocks (C1 and C2), which resulted particularly disadvantageous in terms of excessive solar radiation and wind exposure. The new designs worked on blocks and vegetation in accordance with the basic typo-morphological conditions established in the original master plan. The actions can be summarized as follows:

• The height of the blocks was increased. To ensure greater consistency and integrity with the original design, the main entrance to the Cittadella was identified as the ideal starting point from which to 'bend' the envelope of the blocks beyond this limit. This rotation, even if minimal in relation to the territorial scale of the project (1°), allowed an increase of the height of the N-W blocks still remaining within the 18m limits.

• A new portico was introduced into the courtyards. The mitigating action of this element allows it to respond in a flexible way to the complexity of the temperature zones. Even in this case, the portico interacts with the project on a larger scale than the individual block. Its planned location in the court on the inner edge of the central square defines and accompanies a new footpath. Its height, moreover, maintains the same height (about 6m), measuring the variation of the ground.

• The vegetation in the original master plan was optimised. In particular: the woody species used in the initial project was replaced by a second one characterized by its 20m height and a dense crown. In addition, a row of trees was also introduced into the N-W courts in order to reduce wind speed and protect building facades and public spaces.

The changes made to the initial configuration were analysed and evaluated using the same procedure applied to the original design. The software results confirmed the validity of the planned interventions. The introduction of the portico along with dense vegetation in the most ventilated areas provides greater comfort in outdoor spaces without raising the humidity excessively. Both elements, in fact, protect and shade horizontal surfaces from direct radiation and provide greater wind resistance without obstructing airflow.

Both the greater height of the blocks and the portico protects the courtyards in which the maximum speed now ranges from 0.45 - 1.35 m/s. The introduction of vegetation into the courts reduces the wind speed to about 1 m/s in the open space and the park. The analysis on June 21 confirms an overall reduction of the solar flow on horizontal surfaces, equal to approximately 20%. The decrease is mainly due to the N-W courtyards where, because of the new arcaded walkway, the hours of sunshine per day are reduced by approximately 25-30%. Further confirmation of the results is shown in the comparison of the Olgyay bioclimatic chart regarding the original master plan and the second one. Both charts take into account the two directions of the prevailing winds during the summer (338° e 135°).

*

According to the initial goals, the present project attests once again to the profound climatic and environmental responsibilities of urban morphology, at the same time highlighting its extraordinary potential as a suitable tool for the construction of the efficient city. The role of the form of urban space (and, consequently, urban design) takes the city with increasing force to the heart of EU policies and sustainable development actions. The direct relationship between urban form and local environmental conditions determines the degree of human comfort in urban space and consequently the overall energy requirements and polluting emissions of urban settlements.
From this perspective, the effort of this effort to define a feedback tool through which the microclimatic consequences of new urban configurations are repeatedly verified allows designers not only to compare multiple solutions, but helps the design process move toward a more energy-aware urban form.

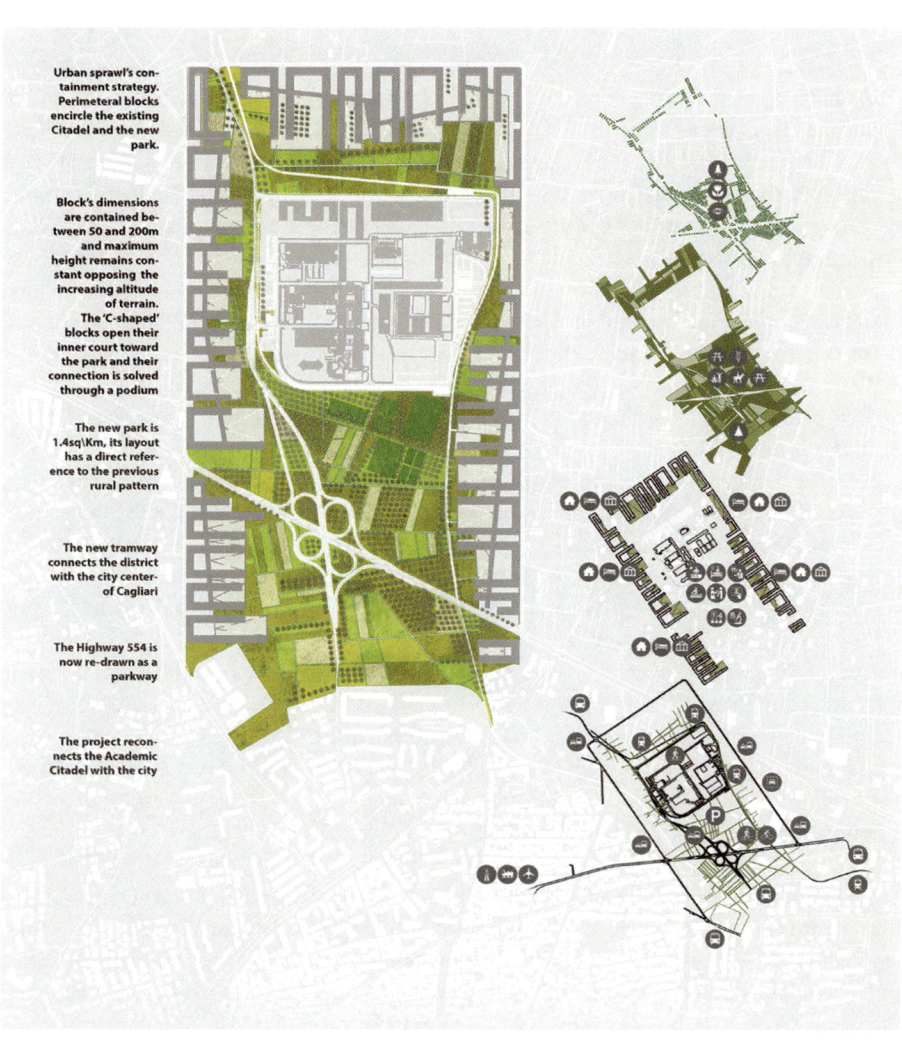

Masterplan

Reasoned bibliography

The bibliography of such a complex and multidisciplinary work is a difficult job in and of itself. The risk of overloading the list with redundant information is great. There are at least three sets of texts that we consulted and studied in depth for the preparation of the articles that preceded this work. The first is made up of general texts that tackle the enormous environmental issues of our century: global climate change, global warming, the energy crisis and the environmental paradigm in global sustainable development policies. These books - some very specialised others more general - provide the references upon which to base approaches and methods of contemporary urban architecture and design. Among them, it is useful to point out some:

- European Commission, Towards a thematic strategy on the urban environment, Brussels 2004;
- European Commission, Thematic Strategy on the Urban Environment, Brussels 2004;
- European Commission, Carta urbana europea II - Manifesto per una nuova urbanità. Strasburgo 2008;
- Butera, F., Energia e sviluppo urbano sostenibile. Archivio di Studi Urbani e Rurali, 2001;
- De Pascali P., Città ed energia. La valenza energetica dell'organizzazione insediativa. Franco Angeli, Milano 2008;
- Droege P., The Renewable City. A comprehensive guide to urban revolution. Wiley&Sons, Chichester 2006;
- Ingersoll R., Questione ecologica in architettura. Lotus, 140, Electa Milano 2009;
- Larsen L., Rajkovich N., Leighton C., McCoy K., Calhoun K., Mallen E., e altri. Green Building and Climate Resilience. Understanding impacts and preparing for changing conditions. University of Michigan; U.S. Green Building Council 2011

The second set consists of a heterogeneous corpus of books, manuals and scientific texts that identify parameters, criteria, methodologies, and protocols for the design of urban elements from the point of view of their relationships with the microclimate. In this case as well, we distinguish more general texts from those that are more technical and specific. Also included are articles by contemporary authors who scientifically approach the study of methods for the environmental control of urban space, benefiting - in their work - from highly advanced techniques and technologies, bringing the discipline to a degree of maturity and control never before attained. Among the most important and significant authors (from which most others draw) we must certainly mention:

- Allard, F., Ghiaus, C., Szucs, A. Natural Ventilation in High-Density Cities. In Designing High-Density Cities. Earthscan, London 2010;
- Breheny, M., The search for a sustainable urban form. The Compact City. E&FN Spon, London 1996;
- Cheng V, Steemers K, Montavon M, Compagnon R. Urban Form, Density and Solar Potential. Clever design and affordable comfort a challenge for Low Energy Architecture and Urban Planning PLEA2006 The 23rd Conference on Passive and Low Energy Architecture. Geneva, Switzerland 2006;
- D'Olimpio, D., La progettazione del microclima urbano, Ed. Kappa, Roma 2008;
- Dessì V, Rogora A. Il comfort ambientale negli spazi aperti. Edicom Edizioni, Gorizia 2005;
- Erell E., Pearlmutter D., Williamson T., Urban Microclimate: Designing the Spaces between Buildings. Earthscan, London 2001;
- Givoni B. Urban design in different climates. World Meteorol Organ WMO/TD. 1989;
- B. Givoni, Outdoor comfort research issues, Energy and Buildings, 2003;
- B. Givoni, Comfort, climate analysis and building design guidelines Original Research Article, in Energy and Buildings, Volume 18, Issue 1, 1992;
- B. Givoni, Man, climate and architecture, Applied Science Publishers, 1976;
- B. Givoni, Climate consideration in building and urban design. Wiley&Sons, New York 1998;
- Landsberg H. The Urban Climate. Academic Press, New York 1981;
- Moonen P., Defraeye T., Dorer V., Blocken B., Carmeliet J. Urban Physics: Effect of the micro-climate on comfort, health and energy demand. Front Archit Res. 2012;
- Ng E., Yuan C., Fung JC., Ren C., Chen L. Improving the wind environment in highdensity cities by understanding urban morphology and surface roughness: A study in Hong Kong. Landsc Urban Plan. 2011;
- Nikolopoulou M., Baker N., Steemers K. Thermal comfort in outdoor urban spaces: understanding the human parameter. sol energy. 2001;
- Oke TR. Boundary Layer Climates. Methuen, 1987;
- Olgyay V., Arquitectura y Clima: Manual De Diseño Bioclimático Para Arquitectos y Urbanistas. Gustavo Gili Barcelona 1998;
- Olgyay V., Bioclimatic orientation method for buildings, J. Biometeor 1967;
- Owens S.E., Energy, Planning and Urban Form. Taylor & Francis, 1986;
- Ratti C., Raydan D., Steemers K. Building form and environmental performance: archetypes, analysis and an arid climate. Energy and Buildings, vol. 1. 2003;

- Ratti, C., Baker, N., Steemers, K. Energy consumption and urban texture. Energy and Buildings, Elsevier, 2004;
- Roaf, S. The Sustainability of High Density. In Designing High-Density Cities. Earthscan, London 2010;
- Santamouris, M. Energy and climate in the urban built enviroment. James & James, London 2001;
- Santamouris, M., Papanikolaou, N., Livada, I., Koronakis, I., Georgakis, C., Argiriou, A., Assimakopoulos, D.N.On the Impact of Urban Climate on the Energy Consumption of Buildings. Solar Energy, Elsevier Science. 2001;
- Santamouris M. Energy and Climate in the Urban Built Environment. James&James. London 2001;
- Steadman P., Energia e ambiente costruito, Mazzotta, 1978;
- Steemers K, Ratti C, Raydan D. Building form and environmental performance: Archetypes, analysis and an arid climate. Energy Build,. 2003;
- Welbank, M. The search for a sustainable urban form, in The Compact City: A sustainable urban form? M. Jenks, E. Burton and K. Williams. E&FN Spon. London 1996

The parts relating to the dawn of the discipline of "climatic urban design" was certainly informed by rereading the canonical texts of urban history and urbanism which, although rarely organized, face the relationships between environmental transformation and the built environment. This group includes the classical treatises from Vitruvius to Alberti and Palladio; reference must be made to them because of the modernity of the concepts expressed. On the figure of Vinaccia, the architect, the sources are scarce and Cesare Silvi's work was of great help along with the direct reading of the author's texts, in particular:

- Aymonino C. L'Abitazione Razionale, Atti dei Congressi CIAM 1929-1930. 4th ed. Marsilio. Venezia 1970;
- Benevolo L. Storia della Città. Vol.3. La Città Moderna. Laterza Editori. Roma 2006;
- Benevolo L. Storia della città. Vol.4. La Città Contemporanea. Laterza Editori; Roma 2006;
- Benevolo L. Storia dell'architettura del Rinascimento. Laterza Editori. Roma 2006;
- De Seta C., La cultura architettonica in Italia tra le due guerre. Laterza 1978;
- Diotallevi I., Marescotti F. Ordine e destino della casa popolare. Milano 1941;
- Harzallah A. Émergence et évolution des préconisations solaires dans les théories architecturales et urbaines en France, de la seconde moitié du XIXe siècle à la deuxième guerre mondiale. University of Nantes. 2007;

- Harzallah A., Siret D., Monin E., Bouyer J. Controverses autour de l'axe héliothermique: L'apport de la simulation physique à l'analyse des théories urbaines. INHA 2014; Available from: http://inha.revues.org/2509
- Hilberseimer L. Großstadtarchitektur. L'Architettura della Grande Città. Napoli 1998;
- Hilberseimer L., Groszstadt Architektur. J. Hoffmann. Stoccarda 1927;
- Heiligenthal RF. Deutsche Städtebau. 1st ed. Heidelberg, Germany: Carl Winter; 1921
- Kratzer FA. Das Stadtklima. 2nd ed. The Environmental Dimension of Urban Design: A Point of View. Braunschweig. Vieweg 1956;
- LeCorbusier. La Ville Radieuse: element d'une doctrine d'urbanisme pour l'equipment de la Civilization Machinist. De L'Architecture D'Aujourd'Hui. 1935;
- Olgyay V. Design with Climate: Bioclimatic Approach to Architectural Regionalism. Princeton University Press, Princeton 1963;
- Rey A., Pidoux J., Barde C. La Science des Plans de Villes. Dunod, Paris 1928;
- Palladio A. I quattro libri dell'Architettura. Hoepli. Milano 1990;
- Pietrogrande E., La casa eugenica e le malattie connesse all'abitazione nei manuali di Diotallevi e Marescotti in La salubrità dell'abitare, Edicom. 2002;
- Plessner H. Die Sonnenbaulehre des Dr. Bernhardt Christoph Faust: Ein Beitrag zur Geschichte der Hygiene des Staàdtebaus. Technische Hochschule. Berlin 1933;
- Silvi C. Solar Building Practices and Urban Planning in the Work of Gaetano Vinaccia (1889-1971). Proceedings of the 2nd International Solar Cities Congress. Oxford 2006;
- Vinaccia G. Il Problema dell'Orientamento nell'Urbanistica dell'Antica Roma. Istituto di Studi Romani. Roma 1939;
- Vinaccia G. La Città di Domani. Come il clima plasma la forma urbana e l'architettura: la sanità e l'igiene cittadina, Vol. 1., Fratelli Palombi Editori, 1943;
- Vinaccia G. Paralleli urbanistici. Confronto della casa a stella con i vari tipi di case in uso, Case d'Oggi, No.9, 1936;
- Vinaccia G. Progetto di casa economica, L'Architettura Italiana, No.10, 1932;
- Vinaccia G. Il corso del sole in urbanistica ed in edilizia. Contributo alla razionalizzazione dell'architettura. Hoepli 1937
- Vitruvio. De Architettura. Einaudi. Torino 1997

Credits

......

The biography of Gaetano Vinaccia that we have sought to trace in this text reveals the multifaceted formation of the architect. His solid competence on the technical issues associated with a sensitivity towards urban and built quality allowed him to reach a synthesis of knowledge that today can only be achieved through the coordination of various expert figures. My thanks go primarily to Ilaria Giovagnorio who, between 2011 and 2016, shared this research in the context of her collaboration with DICAAR. I would also like to thank Maria Grazia Badas and Simone Ferrari for the patience shown in explaining the arcana of fluid mechanics to an architect and for their foresight in wanting to explore a hybrid territory encompassing different disciplines. The contribution and support of Emanuele Mura and Giuseppe Desogus should certainly be mentioned on a par with that of Alessandro Palmas of CONSELF for the use of CFD software on the case studies. Daniela Piga and Elisabetta Pittorru lent their time to the first experiments and Daniela Usai's thesis accompanied the writing of the text on the Roman city. Finally, special thanks goes to the engineer Cesare Silvi for his studies on the Italian pioneer of "climatic urban design" which guided and inspired this work.

The texts and images of this book are by Giovanni Marco Chiri and Ilaria Giovagnorio equally

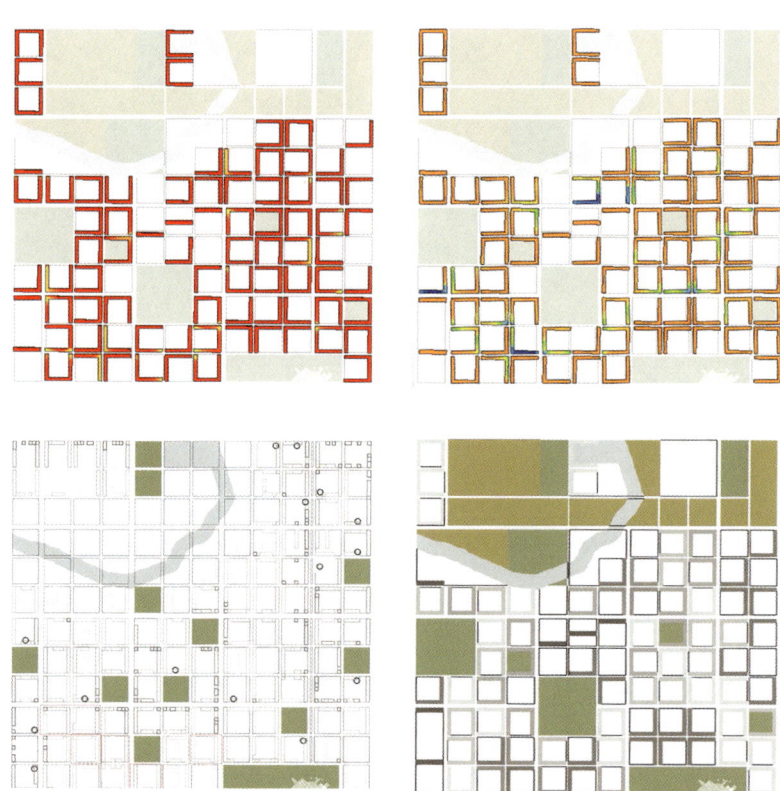

carnet

CLIMATICA
City form

Written by
Giovanni, Marco Chiri
with writings and images of Ilaria Giovagnorio

Author
Giovanni Marco Chiri

Published by
LISt Lab
info@listlab.eu
listlab.eu

Editorial Director
Alessandro Franceschini

Art Director & Production
Blacklist Creative, BCN
blacklist-creative.com

ISBN 9788832080032

Printed and bound in the European Union,
Decembre 2018

Serie back to basics

Prohibited total or partial reproduction of this book by any means, without permission of the author and Publisher.

All rights reserved
© of LISt Lab edition;
© of the author's texts;
© of the author's images;

Promotion and distribution in Italy
Messaggerie Libri, Spa, Milano,
assistenza.ordini@meli.it;
amministrazione.vendite@meli.it

International promotion and distribution
ACC Book Distribution Ltd
Woodbridge, Suffolk, IP12 4SD, UK
sales@antique-acc.com

The Scientific Committee of the issues List
Eve Blau (Harvard GSD), Maurizio Carta (University of Palermo), Eva Castro (Architectural Association London) Alberto Clementi (University of Chieti), Alberto Cecchetto (University of Venezia), Stefano De Martino (University of Innsbruck), Corrado Diamantini (University of Trento), Antonio De Rossi (University of Torino), Franco Farinelli (University of Bologna), Carlo Gasparrini (University of Napoli), Manuel Gausa (University of Genova), Giovanni Maciocco (University of Sassari/Alghero), Antonio Paris (University of Roma), Mosè Ricci (University of Trento), Roger Riewe (University of Graz), Pino Scaglione (University of Trento), Claudia Battaino (University of Trento), Luca Zecchin (University of Trento).

LISt Lab is an editorial workshop, based in Europe, that works on contemporary issues. LISt Lab not only publishes, but also researches, proposes, promotes, produces, creates networks.

LISt Lab is a green company committed to respect the environment. Paper, ink, glues and all processings come from short supply chains and aim at limiting pollution. The print run of books and magazines is based on consumption patterns, thus preventing waste of paper and surpluses. LISt Lab aims at the responsibility of the authors and markets, towards the knowledge of a new publishing culture based on resource management.